HEROES

OF THE

GOODWIN SANDS

BY THE

REV. THOMAS STANLEY TREANOR, M.A.

CHAPLAIN, MISSIONS TO SEAMEN, DEAL AND THE DOWNS

FOURTH EDITION

THE RELIGIOUS TRACT SOCIETY

56 PATERNOSTER ROW, AND 65 ST. PAUL'S CHURCHYARD

1893

From a Photograph] THE BOOM OF A DISTANT GUN. *[by W. H. Franklin.*

R. ROBERTS, *Coxswain, North Deal Lifeboat.*
JOHN MACKINS, *Coxswain, Walmer Lifeboat.*
JAMES LAMING, *Coxswain, Kingsdown Lifeboat.*

PREFACE

—◦—

FOR fourteen years, as Missions to Seamen Chaplain
for the Downs, the writer of the following chapters has
seen much of the Deal boatmen, both ashore and in their
daily perilous life afloat. For ten years he has also
been the Honorary Secretary of the Royal National
Lifeboat Institution for the Goodwin Sands and Downs
Branch ; he has been sometimes afloat in the lifeboats
at night and in storm, and he has come into official
contact with the boatmen in their lifeboat work, in the
three lifeboats stationed, right opposite the Goodwin
Sands, at Deal, Walmer, and Kingsdown. With these
opportunities of observation, he has written accurate
accounts of a few of the splendid rescues effected on
those out-lying and dangerous sands by the boatmen
he knows so well.

Each case is authenticated by names and dates ; the
position of the wrecked vessel is given with exactness,
and the handling and manœuvring of the lifeboat described, from a sailor's point of view, with accuracy,
even in details.

The descriptions of the sea—of Nature in some of her

most tremendous aspects, of the breakers on the Goodwins—and of the stubborn courage of the men who man
our lifeboats are far below the reality. Each incident
occurred as it is related, and is absolutely true.

The Deal boatmen are almost as mute as the fishes
of the sea respecting their own deeds of daring and of
mercy on the Goodwin Sands. It is but justice to
those humble heroes of the Kentish coast that an attempt
should be made to tell some parts of their wondrous
story.

ON THE SANDS.

CONTENTS

—◆—

LIST OF ILLUSTRATIONS

From a Photograph]

THE LAUNCH OF THE LIFEBOAT.

[by W. H. Franklin.

CHAPTER I

'Would'st thou,' so the helmsman answered,
'Learn the secrets of the sea?
 Only those who brave its dangers
 Comprehend its mystery.'

THE Goodwin Sands are a great sandbank, eight miles long and about four miles wide, rising out of deep water four miles off Deal at their nearest point to the mainland. They run lengthwise from north to south, and their breadth is measured from east to west. Counting from the farthest points of shallow water around the Goodwins, their dimensions might be reckoned a little more, but the above is sufficiently accurate.

Between them and Deal lies thus a stretch of four miles of deep water, in which there is a great anchorage for shipping. This anchorage, of historic interest, is called the Downs—possibly from the French *les Dunes*, or 'the Sands,' a derivation which, so far as I know, was first suggested by myself—and is sheltered from the easterly gales to some extent by the Goodwins.

The Downs are open to the north and south, and through this anchorage of the Downs runs the outward and homeward bound stream of shipping of all nations, to and from London and the northern ports of England, Holland, Germany, and the Baltic.

A very large proportion of the stream of shipping bound to London passes inside the Goodwins or through the Downs, especially when the wind is south-west, inasmuch as if they went in west winds outside the Goodwins, they would find themselves a long way to leeward of the Gull buoy.

The passage here, between the Gull buoy and the Goodwin Sands, is not more than two miles wide; and again I venture to suggest that the Gull stream is derived from the French *la Gueule.*

Though there are four miles of deep water between the Goodwin Sands and the mainland, this deep water has rocky shallows and dangerous patches in it, but I shall not attempt to describe them, merely endeavouring to concentrate the reader's attention on the Goodwin Sands. Inside the Goodwins and in this comparatively sheltered anchorage of deep water, the outward bound shipping bring up, waiting sometimes for weeks for fair wind; hence Gay's lines are strictly accurate,

All in the Downs the fleet was moored.

The anchorage of the Downs is sheltered from west winds by the mainland and from east winds by the dreaded Goodwins. They thus form a natural and useful breakwater towards the east, creating the anchorage of the Downs.

In an easterly gale, notwithstanding the protection of the Goodwins, there is a very heavy and even tremendous sea in the Downs, for the Goodwin Sands lie low in the water, and when they are covered by the tide—as they always are at high water—the protection they afford is much diminished.

The 'sheltered' anchorage of the Downs is thus a relative term. Even in this shelter vessels are sometimes blown away from their anchors both by easterly and westerly winds.

In 1703 thirteen men-of-war were lost in the Downs in the same gale in which Winstanley perished in the Eddystone Lighthouse of his own construction, and I have seen vessels in winds both from east and west driven to destruction from the Downs. Even of late years I have seen 450 vessels at anchor in the Downs, reaching away to the north and south for nearly eight miles.

Their appearance is most imposing, as may be judged from the engraving on page 95, in which, however, only twenty-five ships are visible in the moonlight. Almost all the ships in the engraving are outward bound, and some, it may be, are on their last voyage.

Outside, and to the east of this great fleet of vessels, lies the great 'shippe-swallower,' the Goodwin Sands. The sands are very irregular in shape, and are not unlike a great lobster, with his back to the east, and with his claws, legs, and feelers extended westwards towards Deal and the shipping in the Downs. Far from the main body of the sands run all manner of spits and promontories and jaws of sand, and through and across the Goodwins in several directions are numbers of 'swatches,' or passages of water varying in depth from feet to fathoms.

No one knows, or can know, all the swatches, which

vary very much month by month according to the prevalence of gales or fair weather. I shall never forget the sensation of striking bottom in one of those swatches where I expected to find, and had found recently before in the same state of the tide, a depth of six feet. The noise of broken water on each side of us, and the ominous grating thump of our boat's keel against the Goodwins, while the stumps of lost vessels grinned close by, gave us a keen sense of the nearness of real peril. We were bound to the East Goodwin light-ship, and in the path of duty, but we were glad to feel the roll of deep water under our boat's keel outside the Goodwins.

No one therefore knows, or can know, by reason of the perpetual shifting of the sands, all the passages or swatches, either as to direction or depth, of the Good-wins ; but two or three main swatches are tolerably well known to the Deal and Ramsgate lifeboatmen.

There is a broad bay called Trinity Bay in the heart of the Goodwins, out of which leads due north-east the chief swatch or passage through the Sands. It is four or five fathoms deep at low water, and from about three-quarters to a quarter of a mile wide, and it is called the Ramsgate Man's Bight. Close to the outer entrance of this great passage rides, about twelve feet out of water, the huge north-east Whistle buoy of the Goodwins, which ever moans forth in calmest weather its most mournful note.

Sometimes when outside the Goodwins on my way from the North Goodwin to the East Goodwin lightship, we have passed so close to this great buoy that we could touch it with a boat-hook, and have heard its giant

breathing like that of some leviathan asleep on the surface of the sea, which was dead calm at the time. I
have also heard its boom at a distance of eight miles.

I have said this great swatch leads north-east through
the Goodwins—but north-east from what, and how is
the point of departure to be found on a dark night? If
you ask the coxswain of the Deal lifeboat, who probably
knows more, or at least as much about the Sands and
their secrets as any other living man, he will tell you to
'stand on till you bring such a lightship to bear so and
so, and then run due north-east; only look out for the
breakers on either side of you.' It is one thing to go
through this swatch in fair weather and broad daylight,
and another thing in the dark or even by moonlight,
'the sea and waves roaring' their mighty accompani-
ment to the storm.

There are other swatches, one more to the southward
than the preceding, and also running north-east, through
which the Deal men once brought a ship named the
Mandalay into safety after protracted efforts.

Another swatch too exists, opposite the East Goodwin
buoy, being that in which we struck the dangerous
bottom. And yet another, just north of the south-east
buoy, leads right across the tail of the monster, and so
into the deep water of the Downs.

Looking at a chart or reading of these passages, they
seem easy enough, but to find and get through them
safely when you are as low down as you are in a boat,
near the sea level, is very difficult, and as exciting as
the escape of the entangled victims from the labyrinths
of old—unmistakable danger being all around you, and
impressed on both eyes and ears.

B

The whole of the Goodwin Sands are covered by the sea at high water; even the highest or north part of the Sands is then eight or ten feet under water. At low water this north part of the Goodwins is six feet at least above the sea level, and you can walk for miles on a rippled surface cut into curious gulleys, the miniatures of the larger swatches. Wild and lonely beyond words is the scene. The sands are hard when dry—in some places as hard as the hardest beach of sand that can be named. Near the Fork Spit the sand is marvellously hard. On the north-west part of the Goodwins, which is that given in the engraving, it is hard, but not so hard as elsewhere. In all cases it is soft and pliable under water, and sometimes in wading you sink with alarming rapidity.

Recently attempting in company with a friend to wade a very peculiar-looking but shallow swatch—to right and left of us being blue swirls of deeper water, the 'fox-falls' on a smaller scale of another part of the Sands, and exceedingly beautiful—I suddenly sank pretty deep, and struggled back with all my energies into firmer footing from the Goodwins' cold and tenacious embrace.

The Sands reach round you for miles, and the greater swatches cut you off from still more distant and still more extensive reaches of sand. In such solitudes, and with such vastness around you, of which the great lonely level stretch makes you conscious as nothing ashore can do, you realise what an atom you are in creation.

Here you see a ship's ribs. This was the schooner laden with pipe-clay, out of which in a dangerous sea the captain and crew escaped in their own boat, as the

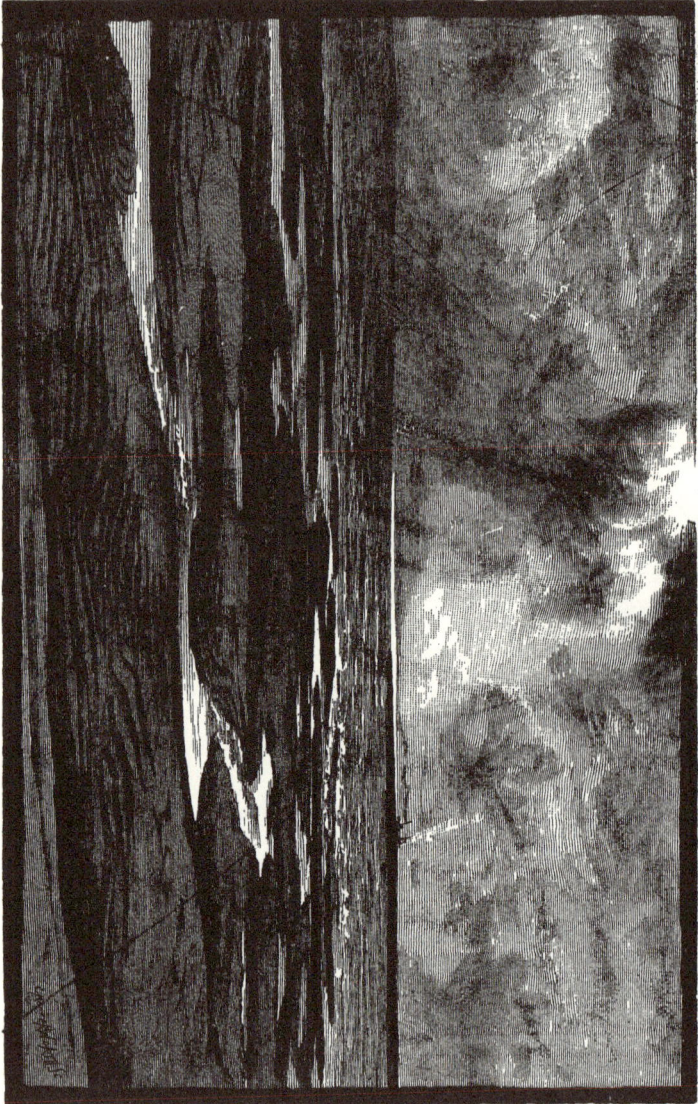

THE GOODWIN SANDS.

lifeboat advanced to save them. Far away on the Sands you see the fluke of a ship's anchor, which from the shape when close to it we recognise to be a French pattern.

With me stood the coxswain of the celebrated Deal lifeboat, Richard Roberts. Intently he gazed at the projecting anchor fluke—shaft and chain had long been sucked down into the Goodwins—and then, after a good long look all round, taking the bearings of the deadly thing, at last he said, 'What a dangerous thing on a dark night for the lifeboat!'

Just think, good reader! The lifeboat, close reefed, flies to the rescue on the wings of the storm into the furious seas which revel and rage on the Goodwins. Her fifteen men dauntlessly face the wild smother. She sinks ponderously in the trough of a great roller, and the anchor fluke is driven right through her bottom and holds her to the place—for hold her it would, long enough to let the breakers tear every living soul out of her!

Under our feet and deep in the sand lie vessels one over another, and in them all that vessels carry. Countless treasures must be buried there—the treasures of centuries. Witness the Osta Junis, a Dutch East India-man, which, treasure-laden with money and other valuables to a great amount, ran on the Goodwin Sands, July 12, 1783. The Deal boatmen were quickly on board, and brought the treasures ashore, which, as it was war time, were prize to the Crown, and were conveyed to the Bank of England [1]. That merchandise, curiosities, and treasures lie engulfed in the capacious maw of the

---

[1] See Pritchard's interesting *History of Deal*, p. 196.

Goodwin Sands is very probable, although we may not quite endorse Mr. Pritchard's statement that 'if the multitude of vessels lost there during the past centuries could be recovered, they would go a good way towards liquidating the National Debt.'

From its mystery and 'shippe-swallowing' propensities, the word 'monster' is peculiarly appropriate to this great quicksand, which still craves more victims, and still with claws and feelers outstretched—Scylla and Charybdis combining their terrors in the Goodwins—lies in ambush for the goodly ships that so bravely wing their flight to and fro beyond its reach. But it is only in the storm blast and the midnight that its most dreadful features are unveiled, and even then the lifeboatmen face its perils and conquer them.

Independently of the breakers and cross-seas of stormy weather, the dangers of the Goodwin Sands arise from the facts that they lie right in the highway of shipping, that at high water they are concealed from view, being then covered by the sea to the depth of from ten to twenty-five feet, varying in different places, and that furious currents run over and around them.

Add to this that they are very lonely and distant from the mainland, and, being surrounded by deep water, are far from help ; whilst, as an additional and terrible danger, here and there on the sands, wrecks, anchors, stumps, and notably the great sternpost of the Terpsichore, from which a few months ago Roberts and the Deal lifeboatmen had rescued all the crew, stick up over the surface. And woe be to the boat or vessel which strikes on these !

On September 12, 1891, on my way to the North

Sandhead lightship, which, however, we failed to reach by reason of the strong ebb tide against us and the wind dropping to a calm, we revisited this sternpost of the Terpsichore. We got down mast and sails and took to our oars. The light air from the north-east blew golden feathery cloud-films across the great blue arch above our heads, and for once in the arctic summer of 1891 the air was warm and balmy. Starting from the North-west Goodwin buoy, we soon rowed into shallow water, crossing a long spit of sand on which, not far from us, a feathery breaker raced. Again we get into deep water, having just hit the passage into an amphitheatre in the Goodwins of deep water bordered by a circle or ridge of sand about three feet under water, over which the in-tide was fiercely running and rippling, and upon which here and there a breaker raised its warning crest.

We reached the great sternpost of the lost Terpsichore at 9.22 a.m., just two hours before low water at the neap tides, and found it projected five feet nine inches above the water, which was ten feet six inches deep in the swilly close to it, but nowhere shallower than eight feet within a distance of fifty yards from the stump. Underneath in the green sea-water there lay quite visible the keel and framework of the vessel; and again I heard the story from Roberts, the coxswain of the Deal lifeboat, who was with me, of the rescue of the crew of this very vessel at 2.15 a.m. on the stormy night of the preceding November 14.

As we held by the green sea-washed stump, it was hard to realise the sublime story of that awful night: the mighty sea warring with the furious wind, and the

dismantled, beaten ship—masts gone overboard and
tossing in mad confusion of spars and cordage along
her side—into which most black and furious hell the
lifeboatmen dared to venture the Deal lifeboat, and out
of which she and her gallant crew came, by God's
mercy, triumphant and unscathed, having saved every
soul on board, and also, with a fine touch of humanity
often to be found in a brave sailor's heart, the 'harmless, necessary cat' belonging to the vessel. I can
assure my readers that poor pussy's head and green
eyes peering out of the arms of one of the storm-
battered sailors as they struggled up Deal beach was a
beautiful and most touching sight.

Having lingered and examined this wreck as long as
we dared, we now tried to get out of the great circle in
which we were enclosed. With one man in the bows
and another steering, we tried to cross the submerged
ridge of sand which encircled us and over which the tide
raced; but we struck the sand, and then were turned
broadside on by the furious current and swept back into
the circle. Cautiously we rowed along, when, not twenty
yards off, I saw an object triangular and not unlike a
shark's fin just above the water. 'Hard-a-starboard!'
at the same moment cried the man in the bows, and
then in the same breath, 'Port, sir, quick! Hard-a-
port!' For to right of us stuck up out of eight feet of
water, beautifully clear and green, the iron pump-work
of a submerged wreck, the iron projection being not
more than six inches out of water; and then, a few
yards further on to the left of the boat, out of deep
water, a rib, it may be, of the same forgotten and it
may be long-buried vessel.

Had not the water been calm and clear, the place would have been a regular death-trap. With increased caution we felt our way all round the great circle into which we had entered. South of us rose a smooth yellow-brown bank of sand, and upon this sunny shore tripped hundreds of great white seagulls. So warm, so silent, so lonely was the place that it might have been an island in the Pacific ; and upon the same yellow sand-bank there basked, quite within view, a great, large-eyed seal.

At last we found our way out of the heart of the Goodwins, and got into the deep, wide swatchway called the Ramsgate Man's Bight. Away to the north-east we saw the Whistle buoy, and toward the east the East buoy, both of which mark the outer edge of the Goodwins.

In the deep centre of this swatch rolled the mast of another wreck, somehow fast to the bottom, and having gazed at this weird sight, we landed, amidst the wild screams of protesting sea-birds, and explored all round for a mile the edges of this sandbank, which was of singular firmness and yellowness, and upon which, in rhythmic cadence, plashed a most pellucid sea.

With change of tide and rising water we got up sail and at last reached the Gull lightship, on whose deck we met old friends, and where we had Divine Service as the evening fell in. Need it be said that that which we had just seen on the Goodwins, the memories of the lost ships, and of the gallant seamen who lie buried there, served to point a moral and to raise all our hearts to that good land where 'there shall be no more death, neither sorrow, nor crying ; neither shall there be any more pain, for the former things are passed away.' One of the hymns in that service was suggested by the scene we had left, and began thus,

Jesus! Saviour! Pilot me.

But not every boat that visits the mysterious quicksand escapes as readily. Skilled and hardy boatmen are sometimes lost even in fine weather.

About twenty years ago a Deal galley punt, and four men, Bowbyas, Buttress, Erridge, and Obree, skilled Deal boatmen, landed on the Goodwins to get some coal from a wrecked collier. All that is certainly known is that they never returned, and that they had been noticed by a passing barge running to and fro and waving, which the bargemen thought, alas! was only the play of some holiday-keepers on an excursion to the Goodwins. They went to the Goodwins in a light south-west breeze and smooth sea. While there the wind shifted to north-east and a tumble of a sea got up, and it is supposed that it then beat into and filled their laden boat, despite the efforts which they are believed to have made to float her or get her ride to her anchor and come head to wind. If this be so, how long and desperate must their struggle have been to save their boat from wreckage, and to pump out the water and heave out the coal. Their anchor and cable, found on the sands and let go to full scope, favours this idea.

On the other hand, the fact that they were seen wildly running to and fro looks as if some sudden catastrophe had occurred, as if they had struck on some stump in the water close to the very edge of the Goodwins.

The very day on which the photographs were taken

A WRECK ON THE GOODWINS.

which have been used to illustrate this chapter, we were shoving off the steep northern face of the Goodwin Sands, when we saw, not ten yards from the precipitous edge of the dull red sands, in about twenty-five feet of water, and just awash or level with the surface, the bristling spars and masts of a three-masted schooner, the Crocodile, which had been lost there January 6, 1891, in a fearful snowstorm, from the north-east, of that long winter. Had we even touched those deadly points, we too should have probably lost our boat and been entrapped on the Goodwin Sands. The coxswain of the Deal lifeboat was with us, and told how that at three o'clock on that terrible January morning, or rather night, wearied with previous efforts, he had launched the lifeboat and beat in the face of the storm and intense cold ten miles to windward, toward the burning flares which told of a vessel on the Sands.

Just when within reach of the vessel, this very wreck, they saw the Ramsgate tug and lifeboat were just before them, and taking the crew out of the rigging of the wreck. In sight of the whole company, for their lanterns and lights were burning, the poor exhausted captain of the schooner, in trying to get down from the rigging, in which he was almost frozen to death, fell into the stormy sea and was lost in the darkness, while the remainder were gallantly rescued by the Ramsgate lifeboat.

It was on the dangerous stumps and masts of this vessel, to save the crew of which the Deal and Ramsgate men made such a splendid effort, that we so nearly ran ; and an accident of this kind perhaps sealed the fate of the four boatmen above mentioned.

On this north-west part of the Goodwins, on which hours of the deepest interest could be spent, you can walk a distance of at least two miles, but you are separated by the great north-east swatch of deep water from getting to the extensive north-east jaw on the other side of the swatch, which is also full of wrecks, and round and along the edges of which, on the calmest day, somehow the surf and breakers for ever roar. The southern part of the Goodwins is also full of memories, and of countless wrecks. The ribs of the Ganges, the Leda, the Paul Boyton, the Sorrento, all lie there deep down beneath the Sands, excepting when some mighty storm shifts the sand and reveals their skeletons. Deep, too, in the bosom of the Goodwins, masts alone projecting, is settling down the Hazelbank, wrecked there in October, 1890 ; but this southern part at lowest tide is barely uncovered by the sea, and only just awash.

At high water the depth is about three fathoms, varying of course in patches, over this southern part or tail of the sea-monster. It is clear that, being thus, even at low tide, nearly always covered with water, and as the sand when thus covered is much more 'quick' and movable, the southern part of the Goodwins is an exceedingly awkward place to explore. If you made a stumble, as the sands slide under your feet, it might, shall I say, land you into a pit or 'fox-fall,' circular in shape, and very deep. The stumps of forgotten wrecks are also a real danger to the boat which accompanies the investigator.

As to the depth of the great sandbank, borings have been made down to the chalk to a depth of seventy-

eight feet—a fact which might have been fairly con-
jectured from the depth of water inside the Goodwins,
down to the chalky bottom being nine or ten fathoms,
while the depth close outside the Goodwins, where the
outer edge of the sands is sheer and steep, is fifteen
fathoms, deepening a mile and a half further off the
Goodwins to twenty-eight fathoms.

The ships wrecked on the Goodwins go down into
it very slowly, but they sometimes literally fall off
the steep outer edge into the deep water above described.

One still bright autumn morning I witnessed a tragedy
of that description.   On the forenoon of November 30,
1888, I was on the deck of a barque, the Maritzburg,
bound to Port Natal.   I had visited the men in the
forecastle, and indeed all hands fore and aft, as Missions
to Seamen chaplain; and to them all I spoke, and was,
in fact, speaking of that only 'Name under heaven
whereby we must be saved,' when my eyes were riveted,
as I gazed right under the sun, by the drama being
enacted away to the southward.

There I saw, three miles off, our two lifeboats of
Kingsdown and Walmer, each in tow of a steamer
which came to their aid, making for the Goodwins, and
on the outer edge of the Goodwins I beheld a hapless
brig, with sails set, aground.   I saw her at that distance
lifted by the heavy sea, and at that distance I saw the
great tumble of the billows.   That she had heavily
struck the bottom I also saw, for crash!—and even at
that distance I verily seemed to hear the crash—away
went her mainmast over her side, and the next instant she
was gone, and had absolutely and entirely disappeared.

I could not believe my eyes, and rubbed them and gazed again and yet again.

She had perished with all hands. The lifeboats, fast as they went, were just too late, and found nothing but a nameless boat, bottom upwards, and a lifebelt, and no one ever knew her nationality or name. She had struck the Goodwins, and had been probably burst open by the shock, and then, dragged by the great offtide to the east, had rolled into the deep water outside the Goodwins and close to its dreadful edge.

What a sermon! What a summons! There they lie till the sea give up its dead, and we all 'appear before the judgment seat of Christ.'

The origin of the Goodwin Sands is a very interesting question, and is discussed at length in Mr. Gattie's attractive *Memorials of the Goodwin Sands*. There is the romantic tradition that they once, as the 'fertile island of Lomea,' formed part of the estates of the great Earl Godwin, and that as a punishment for his crimes they 'sonke sodainly into the sea.' Another tradition, given by W. Lambard, tells us that in the end of the reign of William Rufus, 1099 A.D., there was 'a sodaine and mighty inundation of the sea, by the which a great part of Flaunders and of the lowe countries thereabouts was drenched and lost;' and Lambard goes on to quote Hector Boethius to the effect that 'this place, being sometyme in the possession of the Earl Godwin, was then first violently overwhelmed with a light sande, wherewith it not only remayneth covered ever since, but is become withal (*Navium gurges et vorago*) a most dreadful gulfe and shippe-swallower.'

The latter phrase of 'shippe-swallower' being only

too true, has stuck, and there does seem historic ground to warrant us in believing that in the year named there was a great storm and incursion of the sea ; but whether the Goodwin Sands were ever the fertile island of Lomea and the estate of the great earl seems to be more than uncertain.

But there is no doubt whatever that the theory that the inundation of the sea in A. D. 1099, which 'drenched' the Low Countries, withdrew the sea from the Goodwins and left it bare at low water, while before this inundation it had been more deeply covered by the ocean, is quite untenable, for the sea never permanently shifts, but always returns to its original level. When we speak of the sea 'gaining' or 'losing,' what is really meant is that the land gains or loses, and therefore the idea of the Goodwins being laid bare and uncovered by the sea water running away from it and over to Flanders is absurd.

In all probability the origin of the Goodwin Sands is not to be ascribed to their once having been a fertile island, or to their having been uncovered by the sea falling away from them, but to their having been actually formed by the action of the sea itself, ever since the incursion of the sea up the Channel and from the north made England an island.

There are great natural causes in operation which account for the formation of the mighty sandbank by gradual accumulation, without having recourse to the hypothesis that it is the ruined remains of the fabulous island of Lomea, fascinating as the idea is that it was once Earl Godwin's island home.

The two great tidal waves of different speed which

C

sweep round the north of England and up the English Channel, meet twice every day a little to the north of the North Foreland, where the writer has often waited anxiously to catch the ebb going south.

Eddies and currents of all kinds hang on the skirts of this great 'meeting of the waters,' and hence in the narrows of the Channel, where the Goodwins lie, the tide runs every day twice from all points of the compass, and there is literally every day in the year a great whirlpool all round and over the Goodwin Sands, deflected slightly perhaps, but not caused by those sands, but by the meeting of the two tidal waves twice every twenty-four hours.

This daily Maelstrom is sufficient to account for the formation of the mighty sandbank, for the water is laden with the detritus of cliff and beach which it has taken up in its course round England, and, just as if you give a circular motion to a basin of muddy water, you will soon find the earthy deposit centralised at the bottom of the basin, so the great Goodwins are the result of the daily deposit of revolving tides.

That the tides literally ' revolve ' round the Goodwins is well known to the Deal men and to sailors in general, and this revolution is described in most of the tide tables and nautical almanacks used by mariners, *e.g.* ' The Gull Stream about one hour and ten minutes before high water runs N.E. $\frac{3}{4}$ N., but the last hour changes to E.N.E. and even to E.S.E., and the last hour of the southern stream changes from S.W. $\frac{1}{2}$ S. to W.S.W. and even to W.N.W[1].' Here the reader will distinctly see recorded the great causes in operation

[1] Jefferson's *Almanack,* 1892.

which are sufficient in the lapse of centuries to produce and maintain the Goodwin Sands. But how they came to be called the Goodwin Sands we know not, and can only conjecture. Those were the days of Siward and Duncan and Macbeth, and, like them, the imposing form of the great Earl of Kent is shrouded in the mists and the myths of eight centuries.

He was evidently placed, in the first instance by royal authority or that of the Saxon Witan, in some such position as Captain of the Naval forces of all Southern England, and it is certain that he gathered round himself the affections of the sailors of Sandwich, Hythe, Romney, Hastings, and Dover.

When he sailed from Bruges against Edward, ' the fort of Hastings opened to his coming with a shout from its armed men. All the boatmen, all the mariners far and near, thronged to him, with sail and shield, with sword and with oar.' And on his way to Pevensey and Hastings from Flanders he would seem to have run outside, and at the back of the Goodwins, while the admirals of Edward the Confessor, Rodolph and Odda, lay fast in the Downs.

He appears, by virtue of his semi-regal position—for Kent with Wessex and Sussex were under his government—to have been the Commander of a Naval agglomeration of those southern ports which was the germ, very probably, of the subsequent ' Cinque Ports ' confederation, with their ' Warden ' at their head ; but at any rate he swept with him in this expedition against Edward all the ' Buscarles ' (boat-carles or seamen) of those southern ports, Hythe, Hastings, Dover, and Sandwich. His progress towards London was a triumphant one with his sons. 'All Kent—the foster-mother of the Saxons,' we are told, on this occasion 'sent forth the cry, "Life or death with Earl Godwin!"'

Crimes may rest on the name of Earl Godwin, despite his oath to the contrary and his formal acquittal by the Witan-gemot, and dark deeds are still affixed to his memory, but 'there was an instinctive and prophetic feeling throughout the English nation that with the house of Godwin was identified the cause of the English people.' With all his faults he was a great Englishman, and was the popular embodiment of English or Saxon feeling against the Normanising sympathies of Edward.

In legend the Godwin family, even in death, seem to have been connected with the sea. There is the legend of Godwin's destruction with his fleet in the Goodwin Sands, and there is the much better authenticated legend of Harold's burial in the sea-sand at Hastings. The Norman William's chaplain records that the Conqueror said, 'Let his corpse guard the coasts which his life madly defended.'

> Wrap them together[1] in a purple cloak,
> And lay them both upon the waste sea-shore
> At Hastings, there to guard the land for which
> He did forswear himself.

Tenterden Steeple is certainly not the cause of the Goodwin Sands, and the connection supposed to exist between them seems to have first occurred to some 'aged peasant' of Kent examined before Sir Thomas More as to the origin of the Goodwin Sands. But, as Captain Montagu Burrows, R.N., mentions in his most interesting book on the Cinque Ports, Tenterden Steeple

---

[1] Edith and Harold.

was not built till 1462, and 'was not in the popular adage connected with the Goodwin Sands, but with Sandwich Haven. It ran thus—

> Of many people it hath been sayed
> That Tenterden steeple Sandwich haven hath decayed.'

Godwin's connection with Tenterden Steeple seems, therefore, to be as mythical as his destruction in the Goodwin Sands with his whole fleet, and we are driven to suppose that the connection of his family name with the Goodwin Sands arose either from Norman and monkish detestation of Harold and Godwin's race, and the desire to associate his name as infamous with those terrible quicksands; or that these Sands had some connection with the great earl and his family which we know not of, whether as having been, according to doubtful legend, his estate, or because he must often have victoriously sailed round them, and hard by them often hoisted his rallying flag; or that these outlying, but guarding Sands received from the patriotic affection of the valiant Kentish men the title of 'the Goodwin Sands' in memory of the great Earl Godwin and of Godwin's race [1].

[1] I am reminded by the Rev. C. A. Molony that Goodnestone next Wingham or Godwynstone, and Godwynstone next Faversham, both referred to in *Archaeologia Cantiana*, are localities which probably commemorate the name of the great Earl of Kent. Hasted mentions that the two villages were part of Earl Godwin's estates, and on his death passed to his son Harold, and that when Harold was slain they were seized by William and given to some of his adherents. Mr. Molony mentions a tradition at Goodnestone near Wingham, that both that village and Godwynstone near Faversham were the lands given by the crown to Earl Godwin to enable him to keep in repair Godwin's Tower and other fortifications at Dover Castle.

CHAPTER II

Where'er in ambush lurk the fatal sands,
They claim the danger.

EVER since fleets anchored in the Downs, the require-
ments of the great number of men on board, as well
as the needs of the vessels, would have a tendency to
maintain the supply of skilled and hardy boatmen to
meet those needs. Pritchard, in his *History of Deal*,
which is a mine of interesting information, gives a
sketch of events and battles in the Downs since 1063.
Tostig, Godwin, and Harold are noticed ; sea fights
between the French and English in the Downs from
1215 are described ; the battles of Van Tromp and
Blake in the Downs, and many other interesting his-
torical events, are given in his book, as well as incidents connected with the Deal boatmen.

With the decay and silting up of Sandwich Haven the
Downs became still more a place of ships, and thus naturally was still more developed the race of Deal boatmen,
who were, and are to the present time, daily accustomed
to launch and land through the surf which runs in rough

DEAL BOATMEN ON THE LOOK-OUT FOR A HOVEL.

weather on their open beach; and whose avocation was
to pilot the vessels anchoring in or leaving the Downs,
and to help those in distress on the Goodwin Sands.

Like their descendants now, who are seen daily
in crowds lounging round the capstans, the night was
most frequently their time of effort. In the day they
were resting 'longshore' fashion, unless, of course, their
keen sailor sight saw anywhere—even on the distant
horizon—a chance of a 'hovel.' Ever on the look-out
in case of need, galleys, sharp as a shark, and luggers
full of men, would rush down the beach into the sea in
less time than it has taken to write this sentence.

But until the necessity for action arose a stranger,
looking at the apparently idling men, with their far-away
gazings seaward, would naturally say, 'What a lazy set
of fellows!' as has actually been said to me of the very
men who I knew had been all night in the lifeboat, and
whose faces were tanned and salted with the ocean
brine.

Justly or unjustly, in olden times the Deal boatmen
were accused of rapacity. But the poor fellows knew
no better—Christian love and Christian charity seem to
have slept in those days, and no man cared for the
moral elevation of the wild daring fellows. True indeed,
they were accused of lending to vessels in distress a
'predatory succour' more ruinous to them than the
angry elements which assailed them. In 1705 a charge
of this kind was made by Daniel Defoe, the author of
Robinson Crusoe, and was sternly repelled by the Mayor
and Corporation of Deal; and Mr. Pritchard mentions
that only one charge of plundering wrecks was made in
the present century, in the year 1807; and the verdict

of 'Guilty' was eventually and deservedly followed by the pardon of the Crown.

With the increase of the shipping of this country, and the naval wars of the early part of the nineteenth century, the numbers and fame of the Deal boatmen increased, until their skill, bravery, and humanity were celebrated all over the world. In those times, and even recently, the Deal boatmen, including in that title the men of Walmer and Kingsdown, were said to number over 1000 men ; and as there were no lightships around the Goodwin Sands till the end of the eighteenth century, there were vessels lost on them almost daily, and there were daily salvage jobs or 'hovels' and rescues of despairing crews ; and what with the trade with the men-of-war, and the piloting and berthing of ships, there were abundant employment and much salvage for all the boatmen.

The dress of the boatmen in those days, *i. e.* their 'longshore toggery'—and there are still among the older men a few, a very few survivals—was finished off by tall hats and pumps ; and in answer to my query 'why they formerly always wore those pumps?' I was told, ''Cos they was always a dancin' in them days'—doubtless with Jane and Bess and black-eyed Susan.

There was smuggling, too, of spirits and tobacco, and all kinds of devices for concealing the contraband articles. Not very many years ago boats lay on Deal beach with hollow masts to hold tea—then an expensive luxury, and fitted with boxes and lockers having false bottoms, and all manner of smuggling contrivances.

It was hard to persuade those wild, daring men that

there was anything wrong in smuggling the articles they had honestly purchased with their own money.

'There's nothing in the Bible against smuggling!' said one of them to a clerical friend of mine, who aptly replied: 'Render therefore unto Caesar the things that be Caesar's, and unto God the things that be God's.'

'Is it so? you're right,' the simple-minded boatman replied; 'no more smuggling after this day for me!' And there never was.

But that which has given the Deal boatmen a niche in the temple of fame and made them a part and parcel of our 'rough island story,' is their heroic rescues and their triumphs over all the terrors of the Goodwin Sands.

There was no lightship on or near the Goodwin Sands till 1795, when one was placed on the North Sand Head. In 1809 the Gull lightship, and in 1832 the South Sand Head lightships, were added, and the placing of the East Goodwin lightship in 1874 was one of the greatest boons conferred on the mariners of England in our times.

It is hard even now sometimes to avoid the deadly Goodwins, but what it must have been in the awful darkness of winter midnights which brooded over them in the early part of this century is beyond description.

Nor was there a lifeboat stationed at Deal until the year 1865. Before that time the Deal luggers attempted the work of rescue on the Goodwin Sands. In those days all Deal and Walmer beach was full of those wonderful sea-boats hauled up on the shingle, while their mizzen booms almost ran into the houses on the opposite side of the roadway. The skill and daring of those brave boatmen were beyond praise. Let me give in more detail the incident alluded to in the account of the Ganges.

Fifty-two years ago, one stormy morning, a young Deal boatman was going to be married, and the church bells were ringing for the ceremony, when suddenly there was seen away to the southward and eastward a little schooner struggling to live in the breakers, or rather on the edge of the breakers, on the Goodwins. The Mariner lugger was lying on the beach of Deal, and there being no lifeboat in those days a rush of eager men was made to get a place in the lugger, and amongst them, carried away by the desire to do and to save, was the intended bridegroom.

By the time they plunged into the awful sea on the sands the schooner had struck, and was thumping farther into the sands, sails flying wildly about and the foremast gone. The crew, over whom the sea was flying, were clustered in the main rigging. It was a service of the most awful danger, and the lugger men, well aware that it was a matter of life and death, put the question to each other, 'What do you say, my lads; shall we try it?' 'Yes! Yes!' and then one and all shouted, 'Yes! We'll have those people out of her!' and they ran for the drifting, drowning little Irish schooner. They did not dare to anchor—a lifeboat could have done so, but for them it would have been certain death—and as they approached the vessel and swept past her they shouted to the crew in distress, 'Jump for your lives.'

They jumped for life, as the lugger rose on the snowy crest of a breaker, and not a man missed his mark. All being rescued, they again fought back through the broken water, and when they reached Deal beach they were met by hundreds of their enthusiastic fellow townsmen, who by main force dragged the great twenty-ton lugger out of the water and far up the steep beach. The interrupted marriage was very soon afterwards carried out, and the deserving pair are alive and well, by God's mercy, to this day.

The luggers are about forty feet long and thirteen feet beam, more or less. The smaller luggers are called 'cats.' There is a forecastle or 'forepeak' in the luggers where you can comfortably sleep—that is, if you are able to sleep in such surroundings, and if the anguish of sea-sickness is absent. I once visited in one of these luggers, lost at sea with two of her crew on November 11, 1891, the distant Royal Sovereign and Varne lightships, and had a most happy three days' cruise.

There is a movable 'caboose' in the 'cats' right amidships, in which three or four men packed close side by side can lie; but if you want to turn you must wake up the rest of the company and turn all together—so visitors to Deal are informed. These large boats are lugger-rigged, carrying the foremast well forward, and sometimes, but very rarely, like the French *chasse-marées*, a mainmast also, with a maintopsail, as well, of course, as the mizzen behind. The mainmast is now hardly ever used, being inconvenient for getting alongside the shipping, and therefore there only survive the foremast and mizzen, the mainmast being developed out of existence.

The luggers are splendid sea-boats, and it is a fine sight to see one of them crowded with men and close-reefed cruising about the Downs 'hovelling' or 'on the look out' for a job in a great gale. While ships are parting their anchors and flying signals of distress, the luggers, supplying their wants or putting pilots on board, wheel and sweep round them like sea-birds on the wing.

As I write these lines, a great gale of wind from the S.S.W. is blowing, and it was a thrilling sight this morning at 11 a.m. to watch the Albert Victor lugger launched with twenty-three men on board, in the tremendous sea breaking over the Downs. Coming ashore later, on a giant roller, the wave burst into awful masses of towering foam, so high above and around the lugger that for an instant she was out of sight, overwhelmed, and the crowds cried, 'She's lost!' but upwards she rose again on the crest of the following billow, and with the speed of an arrow flew to the land on this mighty shooting sea.

Just at the same moment as the lugger came ashore the bold coxswain of the North Deal lifeboat launched with a gallant crew to the rescue of a despairing vessel, the details of which service are found below.

There is no harbour at Deal, and all boats are heaved up the steep shingly beach, fifty or sixty yards from the water's edge, by a capstan and capstan bars, which, when a lugger is hove up, are manned by twenty or thirty men. When hauled up thus to their position the boats are held fast on the inclined plane on which they rest by a stern chain rove through a hole in the keel called the 'ruffles.' This chain is fastened by a 'trigger,' and when next the lugger is to be launched great flat blocks of wood called 'skids,' which are always well greased, are laid down in front of her stem, her crew climb on board, the mizzen is set, and the trigger is let go. By her own impetus the lugger rushes down the

LAUNCHING A DEAL LUGGER IN A GALE.

steep slope on the slippery skids into the sea. Even
when a heavy sea is beating right on shore, the force
acquired by the rush is sufficient to drive her safely
into deep water. Lest too heavy a surf or any unfore-
seen accident should prevent this, a cable called a 'haul-
off warp' is made fast to an anchor moored out far, by
which the lugger men, if need arise, haul their boat out
beyond the shallow water. The arrangements above
described are exactly those adopted by the lifeboats,
which are also lugger-rigged, and being almost identical
in their rig are singularly familiar to Deal men. The
introduction of steam has diminished greatly the number
of the luggers, as fewer vessels than formerly wait in
the Downs, and there is less demand for the services of
the boatmen.

There was formerly another class of Deal boats, the
forty-feet smuggling boats of sixty or seventy years ago.
The length, flat floor, and sharpness of those open boats,
together with the enormous press of sail they carried,
enabled them often to escape the revenue vessels by
sheer speed, and to land their casks of brandy or to float
them up Sandwich River in the darkness, and then run
back empty to France for more. In the 'good old
times' those piratical-looking craft would pick up a
long thirty-feet baulk of timber at sea—timber vessels
from the Baltic or coming across the Atlantic often
lose some of their deck-load—and when engaged in
towing it ashore would be pounced upon by the revenue
officers, who would only find, to their own discomfiture,
amidst the hearty 'guffaws' of the boatmen, that the
latter were merely trying to earn 'salvage' by towing
the timber ashore.

D

A little closer search would have revealed that the innocent-looking baulk of timber was hollow from end to end, and was full of lace, tobacco, cases of schnapps, 'square face,' brandy, and silks.   There is little or no smuggling now, and the little that there is, is almost forced on the men by foreign vessels.

Perhaps four boatmen have been out all night looking for a job in their galley punt.   At morning dawn they find a captain who employs them to get his ship a good berth, or to take him to the Ness.   Perhaps the captain says—and this is an actual case—in imperfect English, 'I have no money to pay you, but I have forty pounds of tobacco, vill you take dat?   Or vill you have it in ze part payment?'   The boatmen consult; hungry children and sometimes reproachful wives wait at home for money to purchase the morning meal.   'Shall we chance it?' say they.   *They* take the tobacco, and the first coastguardsman ashore takes *them*, tobacco and all, before the magistrates, and I sometimes have been sent for to the 'lock-up,' to find three or four misguided fellows in the grasp of the law of their country, which poverty and opportunity and temptation have led them to violate.

At present a large number of galley punts lie on Deal beach.   These boats carry one lugsail on a mast shipped well amidships.   These boats vary in size from twenty-one feet to thirty feet in length, and seven feet beam, and as the Mission boat which I have steered for thirteen years, as Missions to Seamen Chaplain for the Downs, is a small galley punt, I take a peculiar interest in their rig and behaviour.

The galley punts are powerful seaboats; when close

reefed can stand a great deal of heavy weather, and are the marvel of the vessels in distress which they succour.

All the Deal boats, the lifeboats of course excepted, are clinker built and of yellow colour, the natural elm being only varnished. And it is fine to see on a stormy day the splendid way in which they are handled, visible one moment on the crest and the next hidden in the trough of a wave, or launched or beached on the open shingle in some towering sea.

I have been breathless with anxiety as I have watched the launch of these boats into a heavy sea with a long dreadful recoil, but the landing is still more dangerous.

If you wait long enough when launching, you can get a smooth, or a comparatively smooth, sea. I have sometimes waited ten minutes—and then the command is given 'Let her go,' and the boat is hurled into the racing curl of some green sea.

Sometimes the sea is too heavy for landing, and the galley punts lie off skimming about for hours. Sometimes if the weather looks threatening it is best to come at once, and then, supposing a heavy easterly sea, you must clap on a press of sail to drive the boat. You get ready a bow painter and a stern rope, and the boat, like a bolt set free, flies to the land. Very probably she takes a 'shooter,' that is, gets her nose down and her stern and rudder high into the air, and, all hands sitting aft, she is carried along amidst the hiss and burst of the very crest of the galloping billow. Fortunate are they if this wave holds the boat till she is thrown high up the beach, broadside on, for at the last minute the helm must be put up or down, to get the boat to lie along the

shore, but only at the very last minute—otherwise
danger for the crew ! I have known a boat landing, to
capsize and catch the men underneath, and I have been
myself tolerably near the same danger.

Three or four men man these galley punts, and the
hardships and perils they encounter in the earning of
their livelihood are great. The men are sometimes,
even in winter time, three days away in these open
boats, sleeping on the bare boards or ballast bags and
wrapped in a sail.

They cruise to the west to put one of their number on
board some homeward-bound vessel as 'North Sea pilot,'
or they cruise to the north and up the Thames as far as
Gravesend, a distance of eighty miles, to get hold of
some outward-bound vessel with a pilot on board, which
pilot is willing to pay the boatmen a sovereign for
putting him ashore from the Downs, and they are towed
behind the vessel, probably a fast steamer, for eighty
miles to Deal and the Downs. I have done this—and it
is a curious experience—in summer, but to be towed in
the teeth of a north-easterly snowstorm from Gravesend
to the Downs is quite another thing ; but it is the common experience of the Deal boatmen. And every day
in winter they hover off Deal in their splendid galley
punts, rightly called ' knock-toes,' for the poor fellows'
hands and feet are often semi-frozen, to take a pilot out
of some outward-bound steamer going at the rate of ten
or fifteen knots an hour. It means at the outside about
5s. per man ; perhaps they have earned nothing for a
week, and hungry but dauntless they are determined to
get hold of that steamer, if men can do it. On the
steamer comes full speed right end on at them. The

Deal men shoot at her under press of canvas, haul down
sail, and lay their boat in the same direction as the flying steamship, which often never slackens her speed the
least bit. As all this *must* be done in an instant, or pale

HOOKING THE STEAMER.

death stares them in the face, it is done with wonderful
speed and skill. While a man with a boat-hook, to
which a long 'towing-line' is attached, stands in the bow
of the galley punt and hooks it into anything he can
catch, perhaps the bight of a rope hung over the steamer's
side, the steersman has for his own and his comrades'
lives to steer his best and to keep his boat clear of the

steamer's sides, and of her deadly propeller revolving astern, while the bowman pays out his towing-line, and others see it is all clear, and another takes a turn of it round a thwart.

The steamer is 'hooked,' and, fast as she flies ahead, the galley punt falls astern, this time, thank God, clear of the 'fan,' into the boiling wake of the steamer, and at last she feels the tremendous jerk—such a jerk as would tear an oak tree from its roots—of the tightening tow-rope.

Then the boat, with her stem high in the air, for so boats tow best, and all hands aft, and smothered in flying spray, is swept away with the steamer as far perhaps as Dover, where the pilot wants to land. Then the steam is eased off and the vessel stopped, but hardly ever for the Deal men.

This 'hooking' of steamers going at full speed is most dangerous, and often causes loss of life and poor men's property—their boats and boats' gear—their all. Sometimes a kindly disposed captain eases his speed down. I have heard the boatmen talking together, as their keen eyes discerned a steamer far off, and could even then pronounce as to the 'line' and individuality of the steamer: 'That's a blue-funnelled China boat— she's bound through the Canal: he's a gentleman, he is; he always eases down to ten knots for us Deal men.'

Even at ten-knot speed the danger is very great, and it is marvellous more accidents do not occur, in spite of the coolness and skill of the boatmen. Accidents do occur too frequently. The last fatal accident happened to a daring young fellow who had run his boat about six feet too close to a fast steamer; six feet short of where he put her would have meant safety, but as it was, the steamer cut her in two and he was drowned with his comrade, one man out of three alone being saved. Just half an hour before he had waved 'good-bye!' to his young wife as he ran to the beach.

Another boat has her side torn out by a blow from one of the propeller's fans, and goes down carrying the men deep with her; one is saved after having almost crossed the border, and I shall long remember my interview with that man just after he was brought ashore, appalled with the sense of the nearness of the spirit land, and just as if he had had a revelation—his gratitude, his convulsive sobs, his penitence. Another man has his leg or his arm caught by the tow-rope as it is paid out to the flying steamer; in one man's case the keen axe is just used in time to cut the line as it smokes over the gunwale before the coil tears his leg off; in another's case the awful pull of the rope fractured the arm lengthways and not by a cross fracture, and the bone never united after the most painful operations.

Owners and captains and officers of steamships, for God's sake, ease down your speed when your poor sailor brethren, the gallant Deal boatmen who man the lifeboats, are struggling to hook your mighty steamships! Ease down a bit, gentlemen, and let the men earn something for the wives and children at home without having to pay for their efforts with their precious lives!

The very same men who work the galley punts I have just described are the 'hovellers' in the great luggers when the tempest drives the smaller boats ashore, and they also are the same men who, in times of greater and extremer need, answer so nobly to the summons of the lifeboat bell.

Pritchard's most interesting chapter, in which the best authorities are quoted at length, is convincing that the word 'hoveller' is derived from *hobelier* (*hobbe*, ἵππος, Gaelic *coppal*) and signifies 'a coast watchman,' or 'look-out man,' who, by horse (*hobbe*) or afoot, ran from beacon to beacon with the alarm of the enemies' approach, when, 'with a loose rein and bloody spur rode inland many a post.' Certainly nothing better describes the Deal boatmen's occupation for long hours of day and night than the expression so well known in Deal, 'on the look-out,' and which thus appears to be equivalent to 'hovelling.'

In 1864 the first lifeboat of the locality was placed in Walmer by the Royal National Lifeboat Institution. In 1865 another lifeboat was placed in North Deal, a cotton ship with all hands having been lost on the southern part of the Goodwins in a gale from the N.N.E., which unfortunately the Walmer lifeboat, being too far to leeward, was unable to fetch in that wind with a lee tide.

This splendid lifeboat was called the Van Cook, after its donor, and was very soon afterwards summoned to the rescue for the first time.

It was blowing 'great guns and marline-spikes' from the S.S.W. with tremendous sea on Feb. 7, 1865, when there was seen in the rifts of the storm a full-rigged ship on the Goodwin Sands. The lifeboat bell was rung, a crew was obtained, and the men in their new and untried

lifeboat made her first, but not their first, daring attempt
at rescue. A few moments before the Deal lifeboat,
there launched from the south part of Deal one of the
powerful luggers which lay there, owned by Mr. Spears,
who himself was aboard; and the lugger was on this
occasion steered by John Bailey. The Walmer lifeboat also bravely launched, and the three made for the
wrecked vessel.

The lugger, being first, began the attempt, and in
spite of the risk (for one really heavy sea breaking into
her would have sent her to the bottom) went into the
breakers. But the lugger, rightly named England's
Glory—and the names of the luggers are admirably
chosen, for example, The Guiding Star, Friend of All
Nations, Briton's Pride, and Seaman's Hope—seeing a
powerful friend behind her in the shape of the lifeboat,
stood on into the surf of the Goodwins to aid in saving
life, and also for a 'hovel,' in the hope of saving the
vessel.

It was dangerous in the extreme for the lugger, but,
as the men said, 'They was that daring in them days,
and they seed so much money a-staring them in the
face, in a manner o' speaking, on board that there
wessel, that they was set on it.'

And when Deal boatmen are 'set on it,' they can
do much.

When the lugger fetched to windward of the vessel
she wore down on her before the wind. She did not
dare to anchor; had she done so, she would have been
filled and gone down in five minutes, so hauling down
her foresail to slacken her speed, she shot past the vessel
as close as she dared, and as she flew by, six of the

crew jumped at the rigging of the wreck, and actually caught it and got on board. The Walmer lifeboat sailed at the vessel and tried to luff up to her, hauling down her foresail, but the lifeboat had not 'way' enough, and missed the vessel altogether, being driven helplessly to leeward, whence it was impossible to return.

In increasing storm and sea, more furious as the tide rose, on came the Deal lifeboat, the Van Cook, Wilds and Roberts (the latter now coxswain in place of Wilds) steering. They anchored, and veering out their cable drifted down to the wreck; then six of the lifeboatmen also sprang to the rigging of the heeling wreck, and the lifeboat sheered off for safety.

The wreck was lying head to the north and with a list to starboard. Heavy rollers struck her and broke, flying in blinding clouds of spray high as her foreyard, coming down in thunder on her deck, so that it seemed impossible that men could work on that wave-beaten plane. She was also lifted by each wave and hammered over the sand into shallower water, so that the drenched and buffeted lifeboatmen had to lift anchor and follow the drifting vessel in the lifeboat, and again drop anchor and veer down as before. All this time three powerful steam-tugs were waiting in deep water to help the vessel, but they dared not come into the surf where the lifeboat lay.

To stop the drift of the wrecked Iron Crown was her only chance of safety, and it would have probably ruined all had they dropped anchors from the vessel's bows, as she would have drifted over them and forced them into her bottom. The Deal men, therefore, with seamanlike skill and resource, swung a kedge anchor clear of the vessel high up *from her foreyard*, and as the vessel drifted the kedge bit, and the bows of the vessel little by little came up to the sea, when her other anchors were let go, and in a few minutes held fast; then with a mighty cheer from the Deal men—lifeboatmen and lugger's crew all together—the Iron Crown half an hour afterwards was floated by the rising tide on the very top of the fateful sands; her hawser was brought to the waiting tug-boats, and she was towed—ship, cargo, and crew all saved—into the shelter of the Downs.

The names of this the first crew of the Deal lifeboat are given below[1], and their gallant deed was the forerunner of a long and splendid series of rescues, no less than 358 lives having been saved, including such cases as the Iron Crown, by the North Deal lifeboat and her gallant crew, and counting 93 lives saved by the Walmer lifeboat Centurion, and 101 lives saved by the Kingsdown lifeboat Sabina, a total of 552 lives have been saved on the Goodwin Sands.

The next venture of the Deal lifeboat was not so fortunate. It was made to the schooner Peerless, wrecked in Trinity Bay, in the very heart of the Goodwins. The men were lashed in the rigging, and the sea was flying over them, or rather at them; but all managed to get into the lifeboat except one poor lad who was on his first voyage. He died while lashed on the foreyard, and was brought down thence by Ashenden, who bravely mounted the rigging and carried down the

[1] Crew of the Deal lifeboat on her first launch to the rescue of the Iron Crown:—R. Wilds, R. Roberts, E. Hanger, G. Pain, J. Beney, G. Porter, E. Foster, C. Larkins, G. Browne, J. May, A. Redsull, R. Sneller, T. Goymer, R. Erridge.

dead lad with the sea-foam on his lips. Among the
rescuers of the Peerless crew were Ashenden, named
above, Stephen Wilds (for many years my own comrade
in the Mission Boat), brave old Robert Wilds, Horrick,
Richard Roberts, and ten others.

I have told of the first rescue effected by the Deal
lifeboat—let me describe one of the last noble deeds of
mercy done on November 11, 1891, during an awful gale
then blowing. In the morning of the day two luggers
launched to help vessels in distress, but such was the
fury of the gale, and so mountainous was the sea, that
the luggers were themselves overpowered, and had to
anchor in such shelter as they could get.

At 2 p.m., tiles flying in the streets, and houses being
unroofed, it was most difficult to keep one's feet ; crowds
of Deal boatmen in sou'-westers and oilskins were ready
round the lifeboat, and in the gaps of the driving rain
and in the smoking drifts of the howling squalls which
tore over the sea, they saw that a small vessel which had
anchored inside the Brake Sand about two miles off the
mainland had parted her anchors, and, being helpless
and without sails, was drifting towards and outwards to
the Brake.

Then the Deal lifeboat was off to the rescue, and with
eighteen men in her, three being extra and special hands
on this dangerous occasion, launched into a terrible sea,
grand but furious beyond description. Hurled down
Deal beach by her weight, the lifeboat was buried in a
wild smother, and the next minute was left dry on the
beach by the ghastly recoil. The coming breaker floated
her, and she swung to her haul-off warp.

Then they set her close-reefed storm foresail and took

WRECK OF THE THISTLE.

her mizzen off. Soon after an ominous crack, loud and clear, was heard in her foremast, and such was the force of the gale that Roberts—the same brave man who, having been second coxswain and in the lifeboat in the rescue of the Iron Crown above described in 1865, on this perilous day in 1891 again headed his brave comrades as coxswain, with his old friend and brother in arms, so to speak, E. Hanger, as second coxswain—hauled down the foresail and set the small mizzen close-reefed on the foremast, and even then the great lifeboat was nearly blown out of the water.

With unbounded confidence in their splendid lifeboat, under this sail, and indeed they can only work their weighty lifeboat under sail, they literally flew before the blast into the terrific surf on the Brake Sand, six men being required to steer her !

By this time the little vessel named The Thistle had struck the Sand, but not heavily enough to break her in pieces, and hurled forwards by a great roller, she grated and struck, and then was hurled forwards again, seas breaking over her and her hapless crew. So thick was the air with the sea spray carried along in smoking spindrifts that the Deal men lost sight of the wreck while they raced into the surf of the Brake.

In that surf—which I beheld from the end of Ramsgate Pier, being called there by imperative business, and thus deprived of the privilege of being with the men—the lifeboat was apparently swallowed up. She was filled over and over again, and sometimes there was not a man of the crew visible to the coxswain, who stood aft steering in wind which amounted to a hurricane, and, according to Greenwich Observatory, representing a velocity of eighty miles an hour.

At this moment I was witness of the fine sight of the Ramsgate tug and lifeboat steaming out of Ramsgate Harbour, brave coxswain Fish steering the lifeboat, which plunged into the mad seas behind the tug, while blinding clouds of spray flew over the crew. Those splendid 'storm warriors' also rescued the crew of the Touch Not, wrecked that day on the Ramsgate Sands; but just while they were steaming out of Ramsgate, away on the horizon as far as I could bear to look against the fury of the wind and rain, struggling alone and unaided in the surf of the Brake Sand, I beheld the Deal lifeboat engaged in the rescue of The Thistle.

There indeed before my eyes was a veritable wrestle with death for their own lives and those of the wrecked vessel's crew. The latter had beaten over the Brake Sand, and was anchored close outside it, the British ensign hoisted 'Union down,' and sinking. Sinking lower and lower, and only kept afloat by her cargo of nuts, her decks level with the sea which poured over them. In the agony of despair her crew of five had taken to their own small boat, being afraid, from signs known to seamen and from the peculiar wallowing of their vessel, that she was about to make her final plunge to the bottom.

But now the great blue lifeboat rode like a messenger from heaven alongside them, and their brave preservers dragged them over her sides into safety from the very mouth of destruction.

Amidst words of gratitude and with praise on their lips to a merciful God, the utterly exhausted crew saw the Deal men set sail and fight their way again through the storm landwards.

Looking back for an instant, all hands saw the appalling sight of the vessel they had left turn on her side and sink to the bottom of the sea.

With colours flying, with proud and thankful hearts they reach Broadstairs, whence I received the coxswain's telegram—'Crew all saved ; sprung foremast. R. Roberts.'

This gallant rescue was effected under the leadership of R. Roberts and E. Hanger, the very same men who were foremost in the saving of the Iron Crown. Their names should not be passed over in silence, nor those of the brave fellows who back up with their skill, their strength, and their lives the efforts of their coxswains.

In very truth the Deal boatmen (Deal, Walmer, and Kingsdown all included) as a class of men are unique. As pilots, boatmen, and fishermen they, with the Ramsgate men, stand alone, in their perils around and on the great quicksand which guards their coast, and they must always be of deep interest to the rest of their fellow-countrymen by reason of their hardships, their skill, and their daring, and above all by reason of their generous courage, consistent with their ancient fame. Faults they have—let others tell of them—but it seems to me that these brave Kentish boatmen are worthy descendants of their Saxon forefathers who rallied to the banners of Earl Godwin and died at Senlac in stubborn ring round Godwin's kingly son.

To them, the lifeboatmen and coxswains of Deal, Walmer, and Kingsdown, friends and comrades, I dedicate these true histories of splendid rescues wrought by them, the ' Heroes of the Goodwin Sands.'

E

CHAPTER III

THE AUGUSTE HERMANN FRANCKE

A brave vessel,
Who had, no doubt, some noble creatures in her
Dashed all to pieces! Oh, the cry did knock
Against my very heart! Poor souls! they perished.

ALL day long April 20, 1886, it had been blowing
a gale from the north-east, and a heavy sea was tumbling on the beach at Deal. On the evening of that
stormy day I was making my way to the Boatmen's
Rooms, at North Deal, where the boatmen were to
assemble for the usual evening service held by the
Missions to Seamen chaplain.

On my way I met a boatman, a valued comrade on
many a rough day in the mission-boat. Breathless with
haste, he could at first only say, 'Come on, sir, quick!
Come on; there's a man been seen running to and fro
on the Goodwins!'

Seeing that immediate help was needed, it appeared
that the coxswain of the lifeboat proposed signalling
a passing tug-boat, and wanted my sanction for the
measure. Had she responded to the signal, she would
have towed the lifeboat to the rescue of the mysterious

man on the Goodwins in an hour or so. As Hon. Secretary of the Lifeboat Branch, I at once authorised the step, and a flag was dipped from Deal pierhead, and blue lights were burned; but all in vain. The tug-boat went on her way, taking no notice of the signals, which it is supposed she did not understand.

It was plain some disaster had taken place, but what had happened on those gruesome sands I could only conjecture until I reached the Boatmen's Rooms. Outside the building I found in groups and knots a crowd of boatmen and pilots, and also Richard Roberts, the coxswain of the Deal lifeboat.

Roberts had that evening, about five p.m., been taking a look at the Goodwins with his glass, a good old-fashioned 'spy-glass.' After a long steady search— 'Why,' said he to the men round him, 'there's a new wreck on the sands since yesterday!' The gale of the morning part of the day had been accompanied by low sweeping clouds of mist and driving fog, and as soon as the curtain of thick vapour lifted, Roberts noticed the new wreck.

The other boatmen then took a look, and they all went up to the high window of the lifeboat-house to gain a better view of the distant Goodwins.

The point where the wreck, or the object they saw lay, was the outer part of the Goodwin Sands towards the north, and was quite eight miles distant from the keen-eyed watchers at Deal.

'That's a wreck since yesterday,' said one and all.

Roberts, gazing through his glass, now cried out, 'There's something, man or monkey, getting off the vessel and moving about on the sand!'

E 2

'Let's have a look, Dick,' said another and another, and then all cried out,

'Yes; it's a man! He's waving something—it's a flag!'

'No, 'tis n't a flag,' said Roberts, 'it's more like a piece of canvas lashed to a pole; it blows out too heavy for a flag.'

Just about the same time, watchers at Lloyd's office had seen through a powerful glass the same object on the Goodwins, and they sent word to the coxswain of the lifeboat that there was a man in distress on the Goodwin Sands, and wildly running to and fro.

The wind, however, being north-east, and the tide having just commenced to run in the same direction as the wind, thus producing what is called a lee tide, it would have been worse than useless for the Deal lifeboat to have launched. No boat of shallow draft of water, such as a lifeboat is, can beat to windward over a lee tide, and had she been launched, the Deal lifeboat would have drifted farther at each tack from the point she aimed at.

As before explained, the Deal lifeboat was unable to attract the attention of the passing tugboat, and it was therefore decided to wire to Ramsgate to explain that Deal was helpless, and ask the Ramsgate lifeboat to go to the rescue.

By an extraordinary combination of misfortunes the Ramsgate lifeboat and tugs were also helpless, and having been suddenly disabled were laid up for repairs. We then anxiously discussed every alternative, and it was sorrowfully decided that nothing more could be done until the lee tide was over, which would be about 10.30 p.m.

It was now dark, and the hour had come for the boatmen's service which I was to hold. The men as usual trooped in, and the room was crowded; the scene was a striking one. Fine stalwart men to the number of sixty were present—free rovers of the sea, men who never call any one master, with all the characteristic independence and even dignity of those who follow the sea. There was present the coxswain of the lifeboat, and there were present also most of the men who manned the lifeboat a few hours afterwards. In every man's face was written the story of dangers conquered, and a lifelong experience of the sea, on which they pass so much of their lives, and on whose bosom a large proportion of them would probably meet death.

On all occasions and at all times those meetings are of overwhelming interest, by reason of the character and histories of each man among that unique audience, and also it may be added on account of their rapt attention to the 'old, old story,' which, 'majestic in its own simplicity,' is invariably set before them. But, on this occasion, add to the picture the distant and apparently deserted figure just seen through the rifts in the mist, 'wildly running to and fro on the Goodwins,' the eager and sympathetic faces of the boatmen in their absolute helplessness for a few long hours—hours that seemed centuries to all of us. Observe their restrained but impatient glances at the clock, and listen to their deep-throated responses to the impassioned petitions of the Litany of the Church of England.

I am only recording the barest facts when I say that the response of 'Good Lord, deliver us,' following that most solemn of all the petitions of the Litany, was touching beyond the power of words to describe. In the midst of the service I stopped and said, 'Has any man another suggestion to offer? Shall we telegraph for the Dover tug?' It was seen after a short discussion that this would be unavailing, and the service went on.

The hymns sung at that service were three in number, and perhaps are familiar to those who read this story :—

Light in the darkness, sailor!
Day is at hand,

being the well-known 'Life-boat' hymn ;

Rescue the perishing ;

and then

Jesu, lover of my soul.

No man present could fail to think at each part of the service, and as each hymn was sung, of the poor forlorn figure seen on the Goodwins, and now in the most dire need of help. Nor do I think that service will ever fade from the memories of those present on that Tuesday evening.

Service over, we all went to the front of the lifeboat-house, and the coxswain and myself once more consulted. We stood just down at the water's edge, where the white surf showed up against the black night, and fell heavily on the shingle, resounding.

We asked, 'Had Ramsgate gone to the rescue?'

'Why was there no flare burning if there were any one or any vessel on the Goodwins?'

'Why the dull oppressive silence and absence of all signs of signals of distress?'

Looking up the beach we saw the black mass of

boatmen all gathered round the door of the lifeboat-house, and we heard their shouts, 'Throw open the doors!' 'Let us have the key!' 'Why not give us the life-belts now?'

Finally we decided to launch at exactly nine o'clock. I went home to dress for the night, having arranged to go in the lifeboat. Meantime the bell was rung, and the usual rush was made to get the life-belts. So keen were the men that the launch was made before the time agreed upon, and the lifeboat rushed down the beach just as I got in sight of her—to my great and sore disappointment—and soon disappeared in the night.

They stood on till they reached the inner edge of the Goodwins, along which they tacked, being helped to windward, and swept towards the north by the weather-tide, which they met about eleven o'clock. As they worked their way into Trinity Bay, a sort of basin in the very heart of the Goodwins, the coxswain felt sure they were drawing near the spot where the wreck had been seen, but it was absolutely dark. They could see nothing, no flare, no light, and they could hear nothing but the hollow thunder of breaking surf.

Roberts now decided to run the lifeboat right through the breakers which beat on the outer part of the sands, and thoroughly to search that part of the Goodwins.

Some said, 'The Ramsgate lifeboat has been here and taken the man off.'

Others, 'If there are people alive on the wreck, why is there no light or flare?'

And then they ran her, in that pitchy blackness, into the surf; she went through it close hauled, and beyond it into the deep sea the other side, and searched the outside edge of the sands, but to no purpose. Then, having shouted all together and listened, they stood back again through the surf, running now before the wind.

The broken and formidable sea raged round the life-boat like a pack of wolves. It broke on both sides of the lifeboat right into her, and literally boiled over her as she flew before the gale and the impulse of the swell astern. Nothing could be seen in this stormy flight except the white burst of the tumultuous waves, and all around was midnight blackness.

Some were of opinion, after the prolonged search, that the wreck had disappeared; but Roberts carried all hearts with him when he said, 'We're not going home till we see and search that wreck from stem to stern!'

Then they anchored in Trinity Bay in four fathoms of water. They each had a piece of bread, a bit of cheese, and a smoke; and with every faculty of sight and hearing strained to the utmost, they longed for the coming of the day.

We may now return to the wrecked vessel, and describe the fate of her captain and crew. She was a Norwegian brig, the Auguste Hermann Francke, bound from Krageroe to sunny San Sebastian with a cargo of ice. She had a crew of seven all told, and the captain's name was Jargersen.

He had been running his vessel that morning before the gale, and at eight o'clock in the forenoon struck on the Goodwins, having either failed in the thick weather to pick up the lightships or the Foreland as points from which to take a safe departure, or being carried out of his course altogether by the strong tides which run around and over the Goodwins, and which, if not allowed for, are a frequent cause of disaster. It was on the shallower northern part of the Goodwins that the Norwegian brig struck in a north-easterly gale.

The brig struck the Goodwins about high water with a terrific crash, and was lifted up by successive billows and thumped down and hammered on the hard sand. Contrary to the popular idea, ships sink but slowly in the sand, which is practically very hard and close. When she took the ground the crew rushed to the main rigging and the captain to the fore rigging. The sea beat in clouds high over the vessel, and the seven men lashed themselves in the rigging to prevent themselves being shaken into the sea by the shocks. Again and again the heavy vessel was lifted up and thumped down; while the weather was so thick that neither could she be seen from the nearest lightship or the land, nor could they on the vessel see the land, or form the least idea as to where they were; conjecturing merely that they were aground on the Goodwins.

At last the mainmast went by the board, carrying with its ruin and tangle of sails, spars and cordage, six of the crew into the terrible billows. As each man unlashed himself he was carried away by the sea before the eyes of the captain. The last of the crew was the ship's boy, who, just as he cast off the fastenings by which he was lashed to the rigging, managed to seize the jib sheet, which was hanging over the side, and called piteously to the captain to save him. A great wave dashed him against the ship's side, and his head was literally beaten in. He too was carried away, and the captain was left alone.

The foremast shortly afterwards gave way, but the captain saw the crash coming, and lashed himself to the windlass, where, drenched and half drowned, he was torn at by the waves which were hurled over the ship for hours.

At last the tide fell, and still, owing to the thick driving mist, no one knew of the tragedy that was being enacted on the Goodwins.

Alas ! many similar disasters take place on the Goodwins, the details of which are covered by the black and stormy nights on which they occur, and nothing is ever found to reveal the awful secret but, perhaps, a few fishermen's nets and buoys, or a mast, or a ship's boat.

With the falling tide the sands round the wrecked vessel became dry for miles, and the captain, half-crazed with grief and terror, climbed down from the wreck and ran wildly about the sands. His first thought was not to seek for a way of escape or help, but to find the bodies of his crew, and to protect them from the mutilations of the sea.

But he found none of them, and then he walked and wildly ran and ran for miles, and waved his hands to the nearest but too-distant lightship. Sick at heart, he then fastened on the wreck a pole with a piece of canvas lashed to it, and, as we know, he was seen by God's mercy about that time at Deal.

As the tide again rose, evening came on, and again the captain had to return to his lonely perch, and to lash himself again as before on the little platform, barely three feet square, over which the sea had beaten so fiercely a few hours before. What visions—what fancies, what terrors may have possessed his soul as the cruel, crawling sea again lapped against the vessel's sides in the darkness of that awful night!

Even now a gleam of mercy shone on him, for though the cold waves again tumbled over and around him, they did not break up the little square platform upon which he stood, and upon the holding together of which his chance of living through the night depended. None may tell of the workings of that man's mind during that long night. It is said that in moments of great peril sometimes the whole course of the past life, past but not obliterated, is summoned up in the most vivid minuteness. Thrice blessed is the man who in that dread moment can trust himself wholly to Him who is 'a hiding-place from the wind and a covert from the tempest.'

And yet, though he knew it not—though hope and faith itself may have burned low, nay, been all but quenched in that poor wearied Norwegian seaman's breast, though grim despair may have shouted in his ears, ' Curse God and die,' all that long night the lifeboat was close to him. The dauntless coxswain and crew, though wearied, drenched and buffeted, were ' determined to see the wreck before they went home.' To use their own simple words, ' They hollered and shouted both outside and inside them breakers, but you won't hear anything—not out there—the way the sea was a roarin'.'

At last morning broke. When the wind is easterly you can always see the coming morning much sooner; and about 3.30, when the birds in the sweet hedgerows were just beginning to twitter, the first soft, grey dawn stole over the horizon in the east.

The weather was clearing fast and 'fining down' when the coxswain roused all hands to 'get up the anchor.' The foresail was set, and then a man in the bows cried out, ' I can see something there—there's the wreck!'—and, indeed, there it was, not more than four hundred yards distant.

Now the sky was lighted up a rosy red, so fast came on the 'jocund morn a tiptoe' over the waves.

'There's a man running away from the wreck!' said the coxswain.

He had descried the bright blue lifeboat with the red wale round her gunwale, and was running to meet her in the direction she was heading. But the lifeboat was making short tacks to windward, and the coxswain taking off his sou'-wester waved it to the running figure to come back and follow the lifeboat on the other tack.

Back again came the solitary man, and then at last was given the final order from the coxswain, ' Run straight into the surf to meet him!' and the lifeboat, carried on by a huge roller, grounded on the sands

Running, staggering, pressing on, the rescued man came close to the lifeboat, and then fell forwards on his knees with face uplifted to the heavens, and his back to the lifeboat.

' They that go down to the sea in ships, that do business in great waters ; these see the works of the Lord, and His wonders in the deep. . . . Then they cry unto the Lord in their trouble, and He bringeth them out of their distresses. . . . Oh that men would praise the Lord for His goodness, and for His wonderful works to the children of men!'

Now rose the glorious sun, darting his golden javelins

high up into the blue majestical canopy; and cheerily into the water, now burnished by the sunbeams, sprang Alfred Redsull, danger and hardship all forgotten, with a line round his waist, to guide and help the exhausted man away from the deadly 'fox-falls,' which were full of swirling water, and at last into the lifeboat. Then with bated breath they learned the story,—that all the rest were gone, and that the captain himself was the solitary survivor. His hands were in gloves; they cut those off, and also his boots, so swelled were hands and feet. They gave him a dry pair of long stockings and woollen mittens, and they let down the mizzen and made a lee for him under its shelter, for he was half perished with the cold of that bitter night. After a few minutes he insisted on again searching the sands for his lost crew, and the coxswain and others of the lifeboatmen went with him.

The lifeboat was by this time high and dry, for the water was falling with great rapidity, and there was a mile of dry sand on each side of her. The company of men now searched the sands, and a long way off the coxswain saw a dark object.

'What's that?' he said.

'That's my ship's rudder,' replied the captain, 'and I walked round it yesterday evening when death was staring in my face.'

Then they came to the wreck; her decks were gone, every atom of what had once been on board her was swept clean out of her: she was split open at her keel, and lay in halves, gaping.

Inside this wrecked skeleton ship lay her foremast, and so crushed and flattened out was the vessel that the men stepped from the sand at once into the hollow shell —and there they saw, still holding together, the little spot of planking, ten feet above them, on which the rescued man had stood, and where he had been lashed : and they took down and brought away as a memento the piece of canvas which he had fastened to the pole, and which had caught the eyes of the boatmen at Deal ; but the bodies of the drowned crew were never seen again.

When the tide rose the lifeboat got up anchor and made for home.   Crowds were assembled at the beach, expecting, as the British ensign was hoisted at the peak, to find a rescued crew ' all saved ' on board ; but, alas ! only one wearied, overwrought man struggled up the beach.

I led him to get some hot coffee and to give him a few minutes' repose ; but he could eat nothing, and he laid his head on his arms and sobbed as if his heart would break for the friends that were gone, and over-whelmed by the mercy of his own preservation.

All honour to the brave coxswain and his lifeboat crew who sought and searched for him through and through that dreadful midnight surf, and stuck to their task with determined resolution, and who found and rescued this poor Norwegian stranger from the very grasp of death !

All honour to the brave ![1]

---

[1] The crew of the lifeboat on this occasion were—Richard Roberts (coxswain), Alf. Redsull, W. Staunton, H. Roberts, W. Adams, E. Hall, P. Sneller, W. Foster, W. Marsh, Thomas May, J. Marsh, T. Baker, R. Williams, G. Foster.

CHAPTER IV

THE GANGES

> I've lived since then in calm and strife,
> Full fifty summers, a sailor's life ;
> And Death whenever he come to me
> Shall come on the wide unbounded sea.

THE rule that gales of wind prevail at the equinoxes
is certainly proved by the exceptions, but October 14,
1881, was an instance of a gale so close to the autumnal
equinox that it belonged rather to the rule than to the
exception. It had been blowing from the west all that
day, and the Downs was full of ships. Others were
running back from down Channel under lower fore
top-sails, all ready to let go their anchors.

Sometimes in stress of weather a ship bringing up
will lose her anchors by not shortening sail sufficiently
before she lets them go. She preserves too much 'way'
through the water, and she snaps the great chain cable
by the force of her momentum as if it had been a pack-
thread.

The wind reached the force of a 'great gale,'—the
entry I find in my diary of that date. The boatmen
say to the present day that it was blowing a 'harricane,'
and, according to the report of the coxswain of the life-

boat, ' it was blowing a very heavy gale of wind.'   There
was, therefore, no mere capful of wind, but a real, whole,
tremendous gale.   Old salts are always ready to pity
landsmen, and to overwhelm them with ' Bless you's ! '
when they venture to talk of a 'storm'; but the harsh,
steady roar of the wind on this day made it plainly and
beyond doubt a storm.

Long lines of heavy dangerous rollers broke on Deal
beach, and only the first-class luggers could launch or
live in the Downs, so great was the sea.   These splendid
luggers being of five feet draught, and having therefore a deeper hold of the water, could do better than
a lifeboat in the deep water of the Downs.   They could
fight to windward better, and would not be so liable to
upset under sail as a lifeboat; but this only applies to
the deep water.

Put the best Deal lugger that ever floated alongside
the present Deal lifeboat, the Mary Somerville, in a
furious sea of breakers on the Goodwin Sands, and the
whole state of affairs is altered.   The lugger would be
swamped and overwhelmed in five minutes, while the
lifeboat would empty herself and live through it successfully.

The fortunes of the vessels in the Downs on that day
were varied.   Some were manfully riding out the gale ;
others were holding on to their one remaining anchor,
signalling for help, and as sorely in need of fresh anchors
and chains as ever was King Richard of a horse.   Some
had lost both anchors and were drifting out to destruction ; destruction meaning the Goodwin Sands, on which
a fearful surf was raging about two miles under their
lee.

One of those driving vessels was the Ganges. She had run back from the Channel to the Downs for shelter, and dropped her anchors running before a strong tide and a heavy gale ; having thus too much 'way' on her, both the long chain cables parted, snapping close to the anchors, and trailed from her bows. Her head was thus kept up to the wind, while there was no sufficient check to her drift astern and outwards towards the Goodwins.

Efforts, but ineffectual efforts, were made to get rid of the trailing cables, and therefore the vessel's head could not be got before the wind, and she could not be steered, but drifted out faster and faster. It is supposed that there was another anchor on the forecastle head, which had somehow fouled, or, at any rate, could not be got loose from some cause or other.

In the confusion, the sails of the great vessel—for she was a full-rigged ship—having been either neglected or imperfectly furled, were torn adrift and blew to ribbons. These great strips of heavy canvas cracked like monstrous whips with deafening noise, thrashing the masts and rigging, and rendering any attempt to furl them or cut them away, perilous in the extreme.

The crew consisted of thirty-five hands 'all told,' of whom the captain, mates, petty officers, and apprentices were English, while the men before the mast were Lascars. Now I think my readers will agree with me in believing that 'Jack,' with all his faults, is a more reliable man to stand 'shoulder to shoulder' with in time of danger than Ali Mahmood Seng, the Lascar. In cold and storm and peril most of us would prefer 'our ain folk' alongside of us.

Some years ago a Board of Trade report contained a

F

quotation from the remarks of a firm of shipowners, to the effect that they largely employed foreign sailors on board their vessels, because they were (*a*) more sober, (*b*) more amenable to discipline, and (*c*) cheaper than British sailors; but they added, 'we always keep a few Englishmen among the crew to lead the way aloft on dark and stormy nights.'

What a heart-stirring comment on the character of the British sailor is there in the passage above quoted! Is there no remedy, and no physician for the frailties and degradations of poor Jack, who, whatever be his faults, 'leads the way aloft on dark and stormy nights?' 'If the constituents of London mud can be resolved, if the sand can be transformed into an opal,' to use the noble simile of a great living writer, 'and the water into a drop of dew or a star of snow, or a translucent crystal, and the soot into a diamond such as

> On the forehead of a queen
> Trembles with dewy light,—

if such glorious transformations can be wrought by the laws of Nature on the commixture of common elements, shall we despair that transformations yet more glorious may be wrought in human souls now thwarted and blackened by the malice of the devil, when they are subjected to the far diviner and far more stupendous alchemy of the Holy Spirit of God?'

The moral to be drawn from these pages surely must be this—that there is splendid material to work upon, the most undaunted heroism and the noblest self-sacrifice, among the seafaring classes of our island.

On this dark, tempestuous night, be the cause what it may, preventible or otherwise, the Ganges drifted helplessly to her fate. A powerful tug-boat got hold of her, but the ship dragged the tug-boat astern with her, towards the Goodwins, until at last the tug-boat snapped her great 15-inch hawser, and then gave up the attempt and returned to land.

The Ganges now burned flares and blue lights for help. Noting her rapid approach to the Goodwins, on which an awful sea was running, and the helpless and dishevelled condition of the vessel, the Gull lightship fired guns and rockets at intervals of five minutes.

This is the proper and recognised summons to the lifeboats, but long before the lightship fired her signal, the Deal boatmen saw the peril of the vessel ; and one of their number, Tom Adams, ran to the coxswain of the Deal lifeboat with the news : ' Tug's parted her, and she'll be on the Goodwins in five minutes ! ' ' Then we'll go,' said the coxswain, and he rang the bell and summoned a crew.

As it was one of the wildest nights on which the Deal lifeboat was ever launched, the very best men on Deal beach came forward to the struggle for a place in the lifeboat, and out of their number a crew of fifteen was got.

R. Roberts, at this time the second coxswain, was afloat in his lugger, putting an anchor and chain on board the Eurydice, and in his absence Tom Adams helped the coxswain to steer the lifeboat, which literally flew before the blast, to the rescue.

The squalls of this tempest were regular ' smokers,' a word which signifies that the crests of the waves were blown into the astonished air in smoking clouds of spray ; and the lifeboat was stripped for the fight, reefed

mizen and double-reefed storm foresail. I should say
that running out before the wind the mizzen was not set,
and they frequently had to haul down the reefed foresail, and let her run under bare poles right away from
the land into the hurricane.

No one can appraise the nature of this dangerous
task who has not run before a gale off shore for five or
six miles to leeward, and then tried to get back home
dead to windwards. No one who has ever tried it, and
got back, will ever forget it, if his voyage, or rather his
escape from death, has been effected in an open boat.

Nor can any one realize how furious and terrible is the
aspect of the sea in a gale off shore, and especially in
the surf of the Goodwins, who has not been personally
through such an experience.

The Royal National Lifeboat Institution pay the men
who form the lifeboat crew on each occasion generously
and to the utmost limit their funds will admit. No one
who knows the facts of the case and the management of
this splendid Institution can have any doubt on this
subject. Each man is paid £1 for a night service, and
10s. for service in the daytime. If he be engaged night
and day, he is paid 30s. This single launch cost £18—
that is, £15 to the fifteen men who formed the crew, and
£3 to the forty helpers who were engaged in launching
and heaving up the lifeboat on her return.

But no money payment could compensate the men
for the risk to their lives—lives precious to women and
children at home ; and no money payment could supply
the impulse which fired these men and supported them
in their work of rescue.

One of the men in the lifeboat on this occasion, Henry

Marsh, and his name will end this chapter, was the man referred to in Chapter II, who had on the day he was going to be married, many years before, rushed into a lugger bound to the rescue of a ship's crew on the Goodwins.

Notwithstanding the splendid services of the Deal lifeboatmen in many a heart-stirring rescue, they seem utterly unconscious of having done anything heroic. This is a remarkable and most interesting feature in their character. There is no boasting, no self-consciousness, and not the faintest word of self-praise ever crosses their lips. The noblest, the purest motives and impulses that can actuate man glow within their breasts, as they risk their lives for others, and they nevertheless are dumb respecting their deeds. They die, they dare, and they suffer in silence.

A lifeboat rescue killed poor Robert Wilds, the coxswain of the Deal lifeboat. The present second coxswain of the same lifeboat, E. Hanger, was struck down after a rescue by pneumonia. J. Mackins, the coxswain of the Walmer lifeboat, was also seized by pneumonia after a splendid service across the Goodwins, when his lifeboat was buried thirty times in raging seas; S. Pearson, once coxswain of the Walmer lifeboat, died of Bright's disease, the result of exposure; and on the occasion of the rescue of the Ganges, one of the crew, R. Betts, had his little finger torn off. The Lifeboat Institution gave him a generous donation. But the rescues by the Deal lifeboatmen are done at the risk, and sometimes at the cost, of their health, their limbs and their lives.

There is a Kentish proverb that 'there are more fools in Kent than in any other county of England,' because more men go to sea from Kent than from any other county in England, Devon coming next; but Kent on this wild night need not have blushed for the folly of her sailor sons, until it be proved folly to succour and to save.

The Ganges had by this time struck on the middle part of the Goodwins, and the sea was breaking mast-high over her. Her lights and flares had gone out, and the lifeboat had the greatest difficulty in finding her. Just when the lifeboatmen were in perplexity, she again burned blue lights, and these guided the advancing boat. When they came close to the wreck they found her head was lying about north, so that the great wind and sea were beating right on her broadside, and a strong tide was also running in the same direction right across the ship.

Just before the arrival of the lifeboat, in the bewilderment of terror, one of the boats of the wrecked vessel was lowered, and one English apprentice and four Lascars sprang into it. In the boiling surf which raged alongside, the boat was upset in an instant, and with the exception of one Lascar, who grasped a chain-plate, all were lost, their drowning shrieks being only faintly heard as they were swept into the caldron of the Goodwins to leeward. There can be no doubt that a merciful insensibility came soon to their relief. To swim was impossible in raging surf, and there would be little suffering in the speedy death of those poor fellows. I once heard a sailor say to another one moonlight night in the Mediterranean, 'Death is nothing, if you are ready for it;' and if there be a good clear view of the country beyond the river, and of the King of that land, as Shep-

herd, Saviour, Friend, the writer firmly holds with his
sailor friend, long since lost at sea. and now with God,
that ' Death is nothing, if you are ready for it.'

The position of the lifeboat had to be now chosen with
reference to tide, wind and sea. Had the lifeboat anchored close outside the vessel, there would have been
the fearful danger of falling masts; and, besides this,

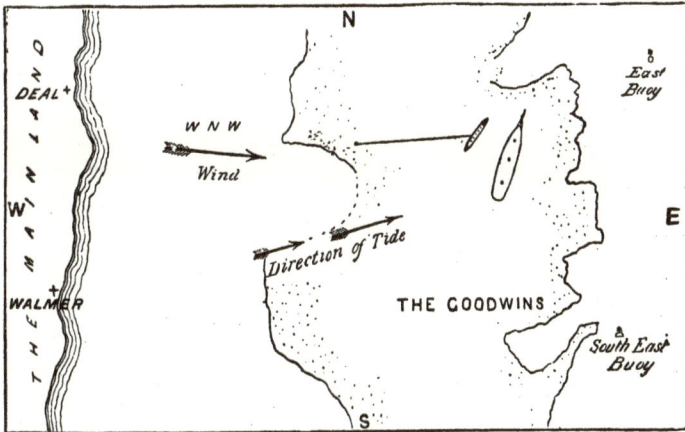

POSITION OF THE GANGES ON THE SANDS.

the tide would have swept her completely away from
the wreck, and would have prevented her getting
back, had she once been driven to leeward; hence,
as shown in the diagram, they were driven to anchor
to windward of the vessel, or right between her and
the land.

They first tried to get to the stern of the vessel, but
they found this position unsuitable, and being baffled,

they hauled up to their anchor with great trouble, and approached the bows of the wreck, having veered out their cable again.

There was, be it remembered, an enormous sea, which during all the struggles of the men broke with fury over the lifeboat, and kept her full to her thwarts all the night, bursting in clouds of spray, and of course drenching the lifeboatmen.

They now got to the bows of the wreck, where the strong off-tide drifted them right under the jib-boom and bowsprit. Looking up, they could just dimly see the jib-boom and bowsprit covered with men, who had, in their terror, swarmed out there to drop into the lifeboat.

As they were hoisted up on the crest of a great breaker, which also filled them, the great iron martingale or dolphin striker of the vessel, pointed like an arrow, came so near the lifeboat that the men saw that a little heavier sea would have driven the spear head of the martingale through the lifeboat. One of the crew had a very narrow escape of being impaled. This novel danger drove them back again therefore to their anchor, to which they had with great difficulty again to haul the lifeboat; and in reply to the imploring cries and shouts of those on the jib-boom, they shouted back, 'We're not going to leave you!'

The lifeboat now lay to windward of the vessel, in the full blast of the tempest, and exposed to the full sweep of the breakers. The official report of the coxswain was: 'We succeeded in getting alongside after a long time and with great difficulty, through a very heavy sea and at great risk of life, as the sea was breaking over the ship.'

As the lifeboat rode to windward of the wreck, the shouts of those on board were inaudible, and their gestures and signs in the dim lantern light could not be understood by the lifeboatmen. Having thrown their line to the vessel, a weightier line was now passed and made fast on board the Ganges, and in order to remedy the confusion and give the necessary directions to save the lives of the distressed sailors, one of the lifeboatmen, Henry Marsh, volunteered to jump into the sea with a line round his waist, to be dragged through the breakers on board the wreck. Heavy seas were bursting on the broadside and breaking over the vessel, so that it was a marvel he escaped with his life.

He fastened a jamming hitch round his waist and then with a shout of 'Haul away!' sprang into the midnight surf. Some said, 'He's mad!' others said, 'He's gone!' and then, 'Haul away, hard!' He fought through the sea, he struggled, he worked up the ship's side, against which he was once heavily dashed, and he gained the deck, giving confidence to all on board: the brave fellow being sixty-five years of age at the time.

The vessel was during this event thumping and beating out over the Goodwins, and was at last, when finally wrecked and stuck fast, not more than one hundred yards from safety and deep water, having thumped for miles across the Sands. The lifeboat had to follow her on her awful journey and almost to the outer edge of the Goodwins.

Her masts had stood up to this time, and she had been listing over to the east, or away from the wind and the sea, but now all over and within the ship were heard loud noises of cracking beams and the sharp harsh snap of timbers breaking. The crew of the wreck, in dread of instant death, now again burned blue lights. Just before the lifeboat approached, as if in a death-throe, the ship reeled inwards, and her tottering masts leaned to port, or towards the lifeboat and against the wind—thus adding great peril to the work of rescue.

By the directions of the coxswain and the lifeboatmen the exhausted crew were at last got down life-lines into the lifeboat, seventeen in number, including the captain, mates and apprentices ; while twelve Lascars got into the Ramsgate lifeboat, which had about this time arrived to help in the work of rescue.

One of the features of this terrible night which perhaps impressed the memories of the lifeboat crew most of all, was the noise of the torn sails above their heads as they fought the sea below. Just before shoving off with the rescued crew, the words of the lifeboatmen were, 'We'll all go mad with that awful noise.'

At last all were on board, thirty-two souls in all, and at two o'clock a.m. the lifeboat got up sail for home, which lay seven miles off dead to windward.

The canvas they set will give some idea of the nature of the struggle—a reefed mizzen and two reefs in the storm foresail. Thus reefed down, they struggled to get hold of the land, which they finally did at four o'clock on that dark wintry morning, landing the rescued men on Deal beach, when boatmen generously took them to their houses [1].

---

[1] The names of the crew of the lifeboat on this occasion were—R. Wilds (coxswain), Thomas Adams, Henry Marsh, T. Holbourn, Henry Roberts, James Snoswell, T. Cribben, J. May, T. May, George Marsh, H. Marsh, R. Betts, and Frank Roberts.

Not the faintest publicity has ever before been given to the details of this gallant achievement, which I now rescue from obscurity and oblivion.

I cannot refrain from recording a previous gallant deed of Henry Marsh, before mentioned. On February 13, 1870, there was a furious tempest blowing, with the wind from E.N.E. All the vessels at anchor in the Downs had been, with one exception, blown ashore and shattered into fragments.

A Dutch brig, sugar-laden, went ashore in the afternoon opposite Deal Castle, and was broken up and vanished in ten minutes; others went ashore at Kingsdown, and late in the evening, opposite Walmer Castle, another brig came ashore, also sugar-laden—a French vessel with an English pilot on board.

The gale was accompanied with snow squalls, and Marsh, hearing of the wrecks along Deal and Walmer beach, determined to go and see for himself. His wife, as is the manner of wives, repressed his rash and impulsive intentions, and said, 'Don't you go up near them!' But Marsh said, 'I'll just take a bit of bread and cheese in my pocket, and I'll take my short pipe with me, and I'll be back soon.' He laid great stress and emphasis on having 'his short pipe' with him, probably reserving a regular long-shanked 'churchwarden' for home use.

He found the beach crowded with spectators, and the sea breaking blue water over the French brig. Her rigging was thick with ice, and the snow froze as it fell. She was rocking wildly in and out, exposing her deck as she swung outwards to the full sweep of the tremendous easterly sea. Between her and the beach there were about ten feet deep of water, which with each giant recoil swept round her in fury.

Marsh asked, 'Are all the people out of that there brig?' 'All but two,' said the bystanders, 'and we can't get no answer from them. They're gone, they are!'

Said Marsh, 'Won't nobody go to save them?'

'Which way are you going to save them?' said one; and all said the same. 'I'm a-going,' said Marsh. 'Harry, don't go!' cried many an old sailor on the beach. 'Here, hold my jacket!' said Marsh. And I verily believe he was thinking chiefly of the preservation of his short pipe. 'Don't you hold me back! I'm a-going to try! Let go of me!' and seizing the line which led from the rocking brig to the shore, Marsh rushed neck deep in a moment into the surf. Swept the next instant off his feet, on, hand over hand, he went; swayed out under her counter, back towards the shore, still he lives! Dashed against the ship's side, while some shout 'He's killed,' up he .clambers still, hand over hand; and as the vessel reels inwards, down, down the rope Marsh slips into the water and the awful recoil. 'He is gone!' they cry. No! up again! with true bull-dog tenacity, Marsh struggles. And at last, nearly exhausted, he wins the deck amid such shouting as seldom rings on Deal beach.

Taking breath, he first fastens a line round his waist and to a belaying pin; and then he discovers a senseless form, Holbrooke, the pilot, a friend of his own, who, fast dying with the cold and drenching freezing spray, was muttering, 'The poor boy! the poor boy!'

'William!' said Marsh. 'Who are you?' was the reply. 'I'm Henry Marsh, and I'm come to save you.' 'No, I'll be lost; I'll be lost!' 'No you won't,' said

Marsh, ' I'll send you ashore on the rope.' ' No, you'll drown me ! you'll drown me !'

And then finding the poor French boy was indeed lost and swept overboard, alone he passed the rope round the nearly insensible man, protecting and holding him as the seas came; and finally watching when the vessel listed in, alone he got him on the toprail of the bulwarks, with an exertion of superhuman strength, and then, with shouts to the people ashore, ' Are you ready?' and ' I'm a-coming !' threw Holbrooke, in spite of himself, into the sea; and both were safely drawn ashore.

The people nearly smothered Marsh when he got ashore, but he ran home, his clothes frozen stiff when he got in; and I have no doubt that the ' short pipe' played no insignificant part in his recovery.

Eleven years afterwards, this same Henry Marsh was dragged by a rope from the lifeboat to the Ganges, as described in the beginning of this chapter, through the breakers on the Goodwin Sands at midnight ; and he is now (1892), my readers will be glad to hear, alive and hearty, at the age of seventy-five, and I rejoice to say ' looking for and hasting unto that blessed hope, and the glorious appearing of the Great God, and our Saviour Jesus Christ.'

There can be few, I think, of my readers who will not find their hearts beat faster as they read this story, and few will hesitate to say, ' Bravely done !'

CHAPTER V

THE EDINA

The oak strikes deeper as its boughs
By furious blasts are driven.

THE Edina was one of a great fleet of ships at
anchor in the Downs on January 26, 1884. Hundreds
of vessels were there straining at their anchors—vessels
of many nations, and of various rigs. There were
picturesque red-sailed barges anchored close in shore,
while even there the sea flew over them. Farther out
were Italians, Norwegians and Yankees, all unmistakable
to the practised eye; French *chasse-marées*, Germans,
Russians and Greeks were there; and each vessel was
characterised by some nautical peculiarity. Of course
the greater number were our own English vessels, as
plainly to be pronounced British as ever was John Bull
in the midst of Frenchmen or Spaniards.

It was blowing a heavy gale from the W.S.W., and
towards night, accompanied by furious rain-squalls and
thunder, the gale increased to a storm. The most
powerful luggers along the beach tried to launch, but
as the tide was high they had not run enough to get
sufficient impetus, and were therefore beaten back on
the beach by the surf.

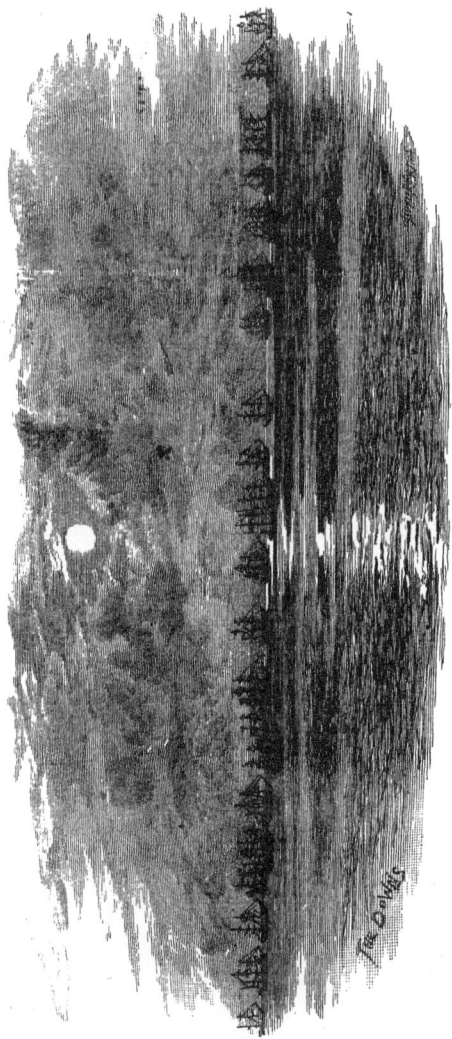

IN THE DOWNS.

Some vessels were blown clean out of the Downs, and away from their anchors. Indeed, when the weather cleared between the squalls, a pitiable number of blue light signals of distress were seen in the distance beyond the North Foreland. And it is probable that vessels were lost that night on the Goodwins of which no one has ever heard.

When the tide fell, about 8.45, flares and rockets were seen coming from the Brake, a very dangerous and partially rocky 'Sand' lying close to the Goodwin Sands. Then the Gull lightship also fired guns and rockets. There being obviously a vessel in danger on or near either the Goodwins or the Brake Sand, the Deal lifeboat bell was rung; and a crew was obtained out of the hundred men who rushed to get a place. The beach was smoothed to give the lifeboat a run, she was let go, and, in contrast with the failure of other boats, launched successfully.

In receiving the report of the coxswain next day, I asked him what time precisely he launched. Now that evening, about 9 p.m., I was sitting in my own house listening to the long-protracted roar of the wind, and just when I thought the strong walls could bear no more, there came a blinding flash of lightning which paled the lamps, almost simultaneously with a peal of thunder that made the foundations of the house tremble. When I asked the coxswain next day what time exactly he launched, his reply was, 'Just in that clap of thunder.'

This may help my readers to depict the scene in its appalling grandeur, and to realise the meaning of the words, 'A vessel in distress,' and the launch of the lifeboat on its sacred errand.

G

The flares which had been burning now suddenly stopped. This, however, was owing to the distressed vessel having exhausted her stock of rockets and torches.

Passing under the stern of a schooner which they hailed, the gallant lifeboat crew were pointed out the vessel that had been burning them, riding with a red light in her rigging to attract notice. Making for her, they anchored as usual ahead, and veered down eighty fathoms. In the gale and heavy sea they found the anchor would not hold, and they had to bend on another cable, and pay out a hundred fathoms, and at last they got alongside.

The captain cried out, 'Come on board and save the vessel! My crew are all gone!' And indeed she was in a sore plight.

That evening after dark, about 6 p.m., this brig, the Edina, had been riding out the gale in the Downs. In a furious blast a heavy sea broke her adrift from her anchor, and she came into helpless collision with a ship right astern of her. Grinding fiercely into this other very large vessel, the Edina tore herself free with loss of bowsprit and jib-boom, all her fore-rigging being in dire ruin and confusion.

In the collision, six of the crew of the Edina jumped from her rigging to the other ship with which they were in collision, leaving only three men, the captain, mate, and boy, on board the Edina. By great efforts they, however, were able to let go another anchor, but that did not bite, and the Edina kept dragging with the wreckage and wild tangle of bowsprit and jib-boom hanging over her bows and beating against her side.

One of the six men who had jumped from the Edina in the panic of the collision had, alas! jumped too short, and had fallen between the two vessels. The next day his body was found by the lifeboatmen entangled in the wreckage, and under the bows of the Edina.

The Edina in her wrecked and crippled condition had dragged till she got to the very edge of the Brake Sand. She had dragged for two miles, and at last her anchor held fast when within twenty fathoms or forty yards of the Brake Sand. She was stopped just short of destruction as the sea was breaking heavily under her stern, and had she drifted a few more yards she would have struck the deadly Brake, and have perished with those on board before the lifeboat could have reached her.

In setting off his rockets, the unfortunate captain had blown away a piece of his hand, and was in much suffering, when the advent of the lifeboat proclaimed that he was not to be abandoned to destruction. The vessel was riding in only three fathoms of water, and as a furious sea was running, she was plunging bows under. Six of the lifeboatmen sprang on board and turned to clearing the wreck—the remainder of the men remaining in the lifeboat, as they feared every moment the ship would break adrift and strike.

They worked with the energy of men working for life, but they took three hours to clear away the wreck; this being absolutely necessary in order to get at the windlass and raise the anchor.

At morning dawn they found the body of the poor sailor who had failed to spring to the other vessel; they got up anchor, they set the sails, and they brought the vessel out of her dangerous position into Ramsgate Harbour.

That day four weeks the Edina came out of Ramsgate refitted and ready for sea. I went on board the vessel on my daily task as Missions to Seamen Chaplain in the Downs, and talked with the captain over the events of the night as here described, and the merciful Providence which prevented him striking on the Brake Sand. 'What brought you up,' I asked him, 'when you had already dragged for miles?'

The captain pointed me to a roll of large-printed Scripture texts, a leaf for each day, for four weeks. 'Why,' said he, 'that's the very leaf that was turned the night of the 26th of last month'—and going close to the 'Seaman's Roll,' as this Eastbourne publication is called—'There,' said he, 'is the very text.'

It ran thus: 'Wherefore, also, He is able to save them to the uttermost that come unto God by Him, seeing He ever liveth to make intercession for them.'

'And that,' said the captain, 'was the anchor that held my ship that awful night.'

It is hard to doubt that He who once stilled the tempest, and granted to this humble sailor the mighty gift of Faith, on that stormy night 'delivered His servant that trusted in Him.'

The Edina went on her way to Pernambuco.

CHAPTER VI

THE FREDRIK CARL

There is sorrow on the sea; it cannot be quiet.

ON October 30, 1885, the small Danish schooner, the Fredrik Carl, ran aground on the Goodwin Sands. She struck on the outer part of the North Sand Head, about eight miles from the nearest land, and two miles from the well-known Whistle Buoy, which ever and always sends forth its mournful note of warning—too often unavailing.

Summoned by the lightship's guns and rockets to the rescue—for the red three-masted North Sand Head lightship was only two miles from the wreck—the Ramsgate lifeboat, towed by the steam-tug Aid, came to the spot, and, after a long trial, failed to get the schooner afloat, and, having taken her crew out of her, returned to the shore.

At low water the next day, October 31, the vessel lay high and dry on the Goodwin Sands. She was tolerably upright, having bedded herself slightly in the sand, and all her sails were swinging loose as the wind chose to sway them. There was no rent in her side that could be seen, and to all appearance she was safe and sound—only she was stranded on the Goodwins, from which *vestigia nulla retrorsum*. As in the Cave of Cacus, once there, you are there for ever, and few are the cases in which vessels fast aground on the Goodwins ever again get away from the great ship-swallower.

The schooner had a cargo of oats, and if she could be got off would be a very valuable prize to her salvors. But 'if'—and we all know that 'there's much virtue in your " if ".'

However, when morning broke on October 31, many of the Deal boatmen, whose keen eyes saw a possibility of a 'hovel,' came in their powerful 'galley punts' to see about this 'if,' and try if they could not convert it into a reality. Accordingly, two of the Deal boats, taking different directions, the Wanderer and the Gipsy King, approached the Goodwin Sands near the north-west buoy.

On this day there was just enough sea curling and tumbling on the edge of the sands to make landing on them difficult even for the skilled Deal boatmen. For the inexperienced it would have been dangerous in the extreme.

There were four Deal men in each boat, and they only got ashore with difficulty, one of the boats' cables having parted; and they had all to jump out and wade waist-deep in the surf, as they dared not let their weighty boats touch the bottom.

Two boatmen remained in each boat, for neglect of this precaution has caused accidents frightful to think of, on the Goodwins ; and the remaining four boatmen, daring fellows of the sea-dog and amphibious type,

From a Photograph]

THE GOODWIN SANDS.

[by W. H. Franklin.

walked across the sands, dripping with the brine. As a matter of fact, two of them were not only Deal boatmen, but were sailors who had been round and round the world, and one was an old and first-rate man-o'-war's man.

Sometimes they met a deep gully with six feet of water in it, which they had to make a circuit round, or to swim ; and farther on a shallow pond, in the midst of which would be a deep-blue ' fox-fall,' perhaps twenty feet deep of sea-water. Then, having avoided this, more dry, hard sand, rippled by the ebbing tide, and then a dry, deep cleft—for the Goodwins are full of surprises— and then came more wading.

Wading on the Goodwins conveys a very peculiar sensation to the naked feet. The sand, so dense when dry, at once becomes friable and quick—indeed, it is hard to believe there is not a living creature under the feet—and if you stand still you slowly sink, feet and ankles, and gradually downwards. As long as you keep moving, it is hard enough, but less so when under water.

The surroundings are deeply impressive. The waves plash at your feet, and the seagull, strangely tame, screams close overhead ; but glorious as is the unbroken view of sky and ocean, the loneliness of the place, and the unutterable mystery of the sea, and the deep sullen roar, and the memories of the long sad history of the sands, oppress your soul. Tragedies of the most fearful description have been enacted on the very spot whereon you stand. Terror, frozen into despair, blighted hope, faith victorious even in death, have thrilled the hearts of thousands hard by the place where you stand, and

which in a few hours will be ten feet under water.   Here
you can see the long line of a ship's ribs swaddling
down into the sands, and there is the stump of the mast
to which the seamen clung last year till the lifeboat
snatched them from a watery grave.

Buried deep in the sands are the cargoes of richly-
laden ships, and their 'merchandise of gold and silver,
and precious stones, and pearls, and fine linen, and
purple, and silk, and scarlet.'   'To dig there' (if that
could be done, say the Deal boatmen), 'would be all as
one as going to Californy;' and who should know the
Goodwins or the secret of the sea better than they do?
'Only those who brave its dangers comprehend its
mystery.'

Keenly intent on getting to the wreck, the four men
hastened on, and they perceived that other boatmen
had landed at similar risk, at other points of the sands,
and were also making for the wreck.

The four boatmen reached the vessel, found ropes
hanging over her side, all sails set, and a part of the
Ramsgate lifeboat's cable chopped off short, telling the
tale of her unsuccessful efforts the night before to get
the vessel off.   They clambered up, and found others
there before them, and soon more came, and eventually
there were twelve boatmen on board.

All eagerly discussed the chances of getting her off.
To the unpractised eye she seemed sound enough ; but,
after a thorough overhaul, some saying she could be
kept afloat, and others the reverse, it was found that the
water had got into her up to the level of her cabin-seats,
and that a bag of flour in one of her cabin-lockers was
sodden with salt-water.   Judging by these signs that the

water would again come into her when the tide rose,
and that she was broken up, the four men whose journey
across the sands has been described, decided with sound
judgment to leave her to her fate, and with them sided
four other men, who also came to the conclusion that it
was beyond the power of their resources to save her.

George Marsh and George Philpot with six others
took this view. Looking overboard, they found the
rising tide just beginning to lap round her.

'Best for us to bolt,' said Marsh; and seeing there
was no time to lose, the eight men came down the ropes
and made for their boats, more than a mile off; leaving
the four others, who took a different view, on board.
The eight men ran, and ran the harder when they found
the wind and sea had increased, and having run and
waded as before half the distance, they made a halt and
called a council of war. There were now serious doubts
whether they would be able to reach their boats, which
they could see a long way off heaving on the swell,
which was becoming heavier every minute.

Some said, 'Best go back to the ship — we'll never
reach the boats.' And indeed it was very doubtful if
they could do either; for the flood-tide was now coming
like a racehorse over the sands, and hiding its fox-
falls and gullies. Others said, 'You'll never get back
to the ship now; there's deep water round her bows
by this time! Come on!'

But some of the men had left brothers on the vessel,
and this attracted three of the company back to the
wreck, and Marsh was persuaded to join the returning
band. And so they parted, there being danger either
way: Marsh with three others back to the ship, and

Philpot with three others to the boats ; and both parties now ran for their lives.

Looking back, they saw Marsh standing in uncertainty, and they waved to him. But he finally decided—little knowing at the time how momentous was his decision —for the ship. He and his party reached it with great difficulty, finding deep water around it, and they were at the last minute pulled on board through the water by lines slung to them from their friends.

Of the others, each man for himself, as best he could, ' pursues his way,'—

And swims or sinks or wades or creeps,

till they all come as close as the rough sea permits them to their boats, and stand breathless on a narrow and rapidly contracting patch of sand.

' Upon this bank and shoal' clustered the four men. The sea was so heavy that the weighty Deal boats did not dare to back into it. The men at first thought of trying to swim to them ; but a strong tide running right across their course rendered that out of the question.

Fortunately a tug-boat hove in sight, bound to the wrecked schooner, and seeing the men waving and their dangerous plight, eased her engines. Deal boats were towing astern, and Deal boatmen were on board, and out of their number Finnis and Watts bravely volunteered to go to the rescue in the tug-boat's punt.

This boat being light and without ballast, they at considerable risk brought off the four men to their own boats, when they forthwith, forgetting past hardship and perils, got up sail for the wrecked schooner, to see how their comrades who had returned, and those who remained on board, were faring.

They found the tug-boat close to the wreck—say half a mile off—and also many other Deal boats; but none ventured nearer than that distance, and none could get nearer.

The wind, which had been blowing from south-west freshly, was dropping into a calm, while great rollers from an entirely opposite quarter were tumbling in on the Goodwins. In fact, a great north-easterly sea was breaking in thunder on the sands, and around and over the vessel. The eight men on board her were therefore beset as if in a beleaguered city, and as nothing but a lifeboat could live for a moment in that tremendous surf, the crews of the Deal boats, astounded at the sight, were simply helpless spectators of their comrades' danger, and torn with distress and sympathy, as they saw them take to the rigging of the vessel.

An hour before this pitch of distress had been reached, a galley punt had gone to Deal for the lifeboat, and in the afternoon, about 3 p. m., the boat reached Deal beach with one hand on board. He jumped out, and staggered up the beach to tell the coxswain of the life-boat that eight boatmen were on board the wreck, and that nothing but a lifeboat could reach the vessel, as there was a dreadful sea all round her, and that his own brother was among the number on board.

The Deal boatmen are not slow to render help when help is needed, and indifference to the cry of distress is not one of their failings; but when they heard of their own friends and neighbours, their comrades in storm and in rescue and lifeboat work, thus beset and in imminent peril, their eagerness was beyond the power of words to describe. From the time the bell rang to 'man the lifeboat' to the moment she struck the water only seven minutes passed!

A fresh south-west breeze brought her to the North Sand Head, and round and outside it to the melancholy spot where, in the waning autumnal light, they could just discern the wreck. They passed through the crowd of Deal boats, and close to the tug-boat; but no one spoke or hailed the other, as all knew what had to be done, and the nature of the coming struggle.

The south-west breeze had now dropped completely, and they encountered, as explained before, the strange phenomenon of a great windless swell from the north-east, rolling in before the wind, which was ·evidently behind it, and which indeed blew a gale next day, though it was now an absolute calm. Great tumbling billows came in from different quarters, and met and crossed each other in the most furious collision. There was tossing about in the sea at the time an empty cask, which was caught in the clash together of two such waves, and was shot clean out of the water as high as the wrecked schooner's mast, or thirty feet into the air, by the force of the blow. The water-logged wreck was now nearly submerged, or just awash, her bulwark-top-rail being now and then exposed and covered again with the advance and recoil of each wave.

Aft there were a raised quarter-deck and a wheel-house, behind the remains of which three of the boatmen took refuge, while the five others climbed into the rigging, but over them even there the sea broke in clouds.

As there was no tide and no wind, it was impossible to sheer the lifeboat, and, whatever position was taken by anchoring, in that only the lifeboat would ride after veering down before the sea. The coxswains, therefore, had to try again and again before they got the proper position to veer down from.

At last, however, they succeeded, and anchoring the lifeboat by the stern, they veered down bows first towards the wreck into the midst of this breezeless but awful sea—bows first, lest the rudder should be injured.

The cable was passed round the bollard or powerful samson-post, and then a turn was taken round a thwart; and the end was held by Roberts, the second coxswain, with his face towards the stern, and his back to the wreck, watching the billows as they charged in line, and easing his cable or getting it in when the strain had passed.

The heavy rollers drove the lifeboat before them like a feather, and end on towards the wreck, till her cable brought her up with a jerk. The strain of these jerks was so great, that, even though Roberts eased his cable, each wave seemed to all hands as if it would tear the after air-box out of the lifeboat, or drag the lifeboat itself in two pieces.

They veered down to about five fathoms of the wreck; closer they dared not go, lest a sea should by an extra strain dash their bows into the wreck, when not one of all the company would have been saved, and the lifeboat herself would have perhaps been broken up.

Then they saw their friends and comrades and heard them cry, 'Try to save us if you can!' And the men said afterwards, 'We got in such a flurry to save them, that what we did in a minute we thought took us an hour.'

At last the cane and lead were thrown from the lifeboat by a stalwart boatman standing in the bows. A heavier line was then drawn on board by the light cane line, and the boatmen came down from the rigging, and, having made themselves fast to pins and staunchions, sheltered behind the bulwark and the wheel-house, seeing the approach of rescue.

Enough of the slack of the weightier line was kept on board the wreck—the end being there made fast—to permit the middle of the rope being fastened round a man and of his being dragged away from the wreck through the sea into the lifeboat. A clove-hitch was put by George Marsh over the shoulders of the first man, who watched his chance for 'a smooth,' jumped into the waves, and, after a long struggle—for the line fouled—was hauled safe into the lifeboat. Marsh on the wreck saw after this that the line was clear, and that no kink or knot stopped its running freely.

Reading these lines in our quiet homes, and in a comfortable arm-chair by the fireside, it is hard to realise the position of those eight boatmen. They were drenched and buried in each wallowing sea, which strove to tear them from the pin to which each man was belayed by the line round his waist ; and their ears were stunned with the bellow of each bursting wave. But, on the other hand, their eyes beheld the grand and cheering spectacle of their brethren in the lifeboat struggling manfully with death for their sakes, and they heard their undaunted shouts.

If for a moment they cast off or lengthened their life-lines, they were washed all over the slippery deck ; and brave George Marsh, who was specially active, was bleeding from a cut on his forehead, having been dashed against a corner of the wheel-house.

The wheel-house up to this time had afforded some shelter to the men who ventured on the deck of the wreck, lashed as just explained, of course, to some pin or bollard; and even they had now and then to rush up the rigging when a weighter wave was seen coming. But just at this time a great mass of water advanced and wallowed clean over the wreck, carrying the wheel-house away with it, and bursting, where it struck the masts and booms, into a cloud : it was too solid to burst much, but it just 'wallowed' over the wreck.

Successive seas are, of course, unlike in height, volume, and demeanour. One comes on board and falls with a solid, heavy lop — there may be twenty tons of blue water in it—the next rushes along with wild speed and fury.

Roberts in the lifeboat now saw a great roller of the latter description advancing ; ready to ease his cable, he cried, 'Look out ! Look out ! Hold on, my lads !'

But before Wilds, the coxswain, who was not a young man, could turn round and grasp a thwart, the sea was on him, and drove him with great force against the samson-post, breaking over and covering the lifeboat fore and aft in fury. This sea would have washed every man off the wreck if they had not had ropes round their waists, and fastened themselves to something ; and it most certainly stupefied them and half-drowned them, fastened as they were.

The blow which Wilds in the lifeboat received would have killed him but that he was wearing his thick cork life-belt. His health was so much affected that he never came afloat again, and he never recovered the strain, the

H

shock, and the exposure of this day. He was a brave man, and a stout, honest Englishman.

> Faithful below he did his duty,
> And now he's gone aloft.

And the writer has good reason for sure and certain hope that this is so. His post as coxswain has since been filled, and nobly filled, by R. Roberts, for many years second coxswain.

In meeting this sea, which struck down poor Wilds with such force, the lifeboat stood straight up on her stern and reared, as the men expressed it, 'like a vicious horse'; and so much did the cable spring, that the lifeboat was driven to within a fathom, or six feet, of the wreck, and was withdrawn the next instant to fifteen fathoms distance by the recoil of the cable.

One by one the men were dragged through the breakers into the lifeboat, until at last only two remained on the wreck, George Marsh and another man. It was Marsh, it will be remembered, who in the earlier part of the day had been persuaded to return to the wreck across the sand, and it was Marsh now who in each case had passed the clove-hitch round his comrades, sending them before himself. He was a very smart sailor and a brave man, and with wise forethought he had also passed the end of the veering line, on which the men were dragged through the surf, over the main boom of the wreck, to let it run out clear of anything which might have caught it ; and, in fact, was the leader of the men in peril on the wreck.

The last two men intended to come together, when another great billow, notice of its advance being given by Tom Adams, came towering and seething, filled the lifeboat, as usual, and covered the ship—indeed, breaking right into her fore-top-sail! That is, thirty feet above her deck!

When the sea passed, the two remaining men, who had been tied together, were not to be seen.

The men in the lifeboat pulled at the line, but it was somehow and somewhere fast to something. And then they shouted, and minutes went by, hours as it seemed to them. At last one of the men—but not Marsh—slowly raised his head and seemed to move about in a dazed condition.

'Where's Marsh?' cried the lifeboatmen.

'Can't find him!' he replied.

'Is he drowned?'

'Is he washed away?'

And the reply was, 'I can't find him.'

And then this man was pulled into the water, and was the last man saved—and that with great difficulty, for the line fouled and jammed—from the wreck of the Fredrik Carl, which had proved a death-trap to poor Marsh, and so nearly to the seven others who were saved.

Still the lifeboat waited in the gathering darkness, and hailed the wreck, hoping against hope to see Marsh appear; but he was never seen again alive. Short as was the distance between the lifeboat and the wreck, it was impossible to swim to her, lying broadside as she was to the swell. Anyone attempting it would either have been dashed to pieces against her, or lifted bodily over her, brained very possibly, and certainly washed away to leeward, return from which would have been, even for an uninjured man, impossible.

And still the lifeboatmen waited and called ; but there was no answer. Poor Marsh had been suddenly summoned to meet his God. The oldest man of the number, and for some years a staunch total abstainer, he had manfully stuck to his post, he had sent the others before himself, and had shown throughout a fine spirit of self-sacrifice worthy of the best traditions of the Deal boatmen.

Slowly and sadly the lifeboat got her anchor up, and never perhaps did the celebrated Deal lifeboat return with a more mournful crew ; for they had seen, in spite of their best efforts, one of their comrades perish before their eyes.

The next day it blew a gale of wind from the northeast, and it was not till several days afterwards that Marsh's body was recovered, entangled in the wreckage, to leeward of the vessel, and sorely mangled. Wrapped in a sail, and with the rope still round him which ought to have drawn him into safety, lay the poor 'body of humiliation' in which had once dwelt a gallant spirit ; but a good hope burned within me as the triumphant lines rang in my ears—

> Deathless principle, arise !
> Soar, thou native of the skies.
> Pearl of price, by Jesus bought,
> To His glorious likeness wrought !

In telling the story of this gallant struggle to save their comrades, made by the Deal lifeboatmen, I lay this tribute of hope and regard on the grave of brave George Marsh.

From a Photograph]　　　'ALL HANDS IN THE LIFEBOAT!'　　　[by W. H. Franklin.

CHAPTER VII

THE GOLDEN ISLAND

Nor toil nor hazard nor distress appear
To sink the seamen with unmanly fear;
Though their firm hearts no pageant-honour boast,
They scorn the wretch that trembles in his post.

THE smart and trim three-masted schooner, the Golden Island, was bound from Antwerp to Liverpool, with a cargo of glass-sand, and was running before a favouring gale to the southward. At midnight, on May 14, 1887, or the early morning of May 15, with a heavy sea rolling from the N.E., suddenly, no notice being given and no alarm felt, she struck with tremendous force the outer edge of the Goodwin Sands.

The timbers of the Golden Island opened with the crash, and she filled, and never lifted or thumped, but lay swept by each billow, like a rock at half-tide, immovable by reason of her heavy cargo. Her crew consisted of seven all told, including a lad, the captain's son, and they managed to light a large flare, which was seen a long way, and was visible even in Deal, eight miles distant.

With what sinking of heart, as the waters raged round

and over them, they watched the flame of their torch burning lower and lower. How intense the darkness when it was extinguished! How terrible the thunderous roar of the breakers!

The nearest lightship was about four miles from them, and her look-out man noticed the flare and fired the signal guns of distress, and sent up the usual rockets.

At 2 a.m. the coastguard on Deal beach called the coxswain of the lifeboat, R. Roberts. Hastily dressing himself he went up the beach, and seeing the flash of the distant guns, he rang the lifeboat bell. Men sprang out of their warm beds, and, half-dressed, rushed to the lifeboat. Their wives or mothers or daughters followed with the remainder of their clothes, their sea boots, or jackets or mufflers. Then came the struggle to gain a place in the lifeboat, and then the bustle and hurry of preparation to get her ready for the launch.

Deal beach at such a time is full of boatmen, some in the lifeboat loosing sails and setting the mizzen, some easing her down to the top of the slope, some seeing to the haul-off warp, a matter of life or death in such a heavy sea dead on shore; others laying down the well-greased 'skids' for the lifeboat to run on, and others clearing away the shingle which successive tides had gathered in front of her bows.

Mingling among the workers are the wives and mothers, putting a piece of bread and cheese in Tom's pocket or helping on 'father' with his oilskin jacket or his sou'wester. And now ' All hands in the lifeboat!' and twenty minutes after the bell is rung she rushes down the steep and plunges into the surf. The loving, lingering watchers on the beach just see her foresail hoisted, and she vanishes into the night, as the green rocket shoots one hundred yards into the sky to tell the distressed sailors 'The lifeboat is launched and on her way.'

The vessel's flare had now burned out, and the guns and rockets from the lightships had ceased, and in front of the lifeboat was only the chill night, 'black as a wolf's throat.' As they worked away from the shore there came in, borne landwards and towards them by the gale, the dull deep roar of the surf on the Goodwins.

It is marvellous how far the sound of the sea on the Goodwins travels. Previously, on a fine calm day, with light breeze, I was standing across the Goodwins, bound to the East Goodwin lightship, and we could hear the roar of the ripple on the Goodwins—not breakers, but ripple—at a distance of two miles. We were sucked into that ugly-looking ripple by an irresistible current, and after an anxious half-hour we got through safely.

In front of the lifeboat on this night was no mere ripple, but breakers; and the deep hollow roar foretold a tremendous sea.

As the dawn came faintly, the breakers were seen by the oncoming lifeboat; she was already stripped for the fight, and her canvas was shortened to reefed mizzen and reefed storm-foresail. Even then she was pressed down by the blast and leaned over as the spray flew mast-high over her. There was a mile of this surf to go through, and with her red sails flat as a board the lifeboat plunged into it.

She thrashed her way nobly through, now up and down on short wicked-looking chopping seas, now on some giant wave hoisted up to the sky; and still up as if she was about to take flight into the air—as we once before experienced in a gale on the Brake Sand—then buried and smothered; and then over the next wave like a seabird. On to the rescue flew the lifeboat, steered by the coxswain himself, beating to windward splendidly, as if conscious of and proud of the sacred task before her. On triumphantly through and over the breakers, onwards to the Golden Island the lifeboat beat out against the sea and the storm. She stood on till quite across the Goodwins, and fetched the East Buoy, which lies in deep water well outside the breakers. In that deep water of fifteen fathoms there were of course no breakers, only a long roll and heavy sea; but the moment this heavy sea touched the Goodwin Sands it broke with the utmost fury, and was sweeping over the Golden Island, now not more than half-a-mile from the lifeboat. At the East Buoy the lifeboat put about on the other tack, and stood in towards the Goodwins and again right into the breakers, from which she had just emerged.

The wreck was lying with her head to the N.W., and was leaning to port, so that her starboard quarter was exposed to the full fetch of the easterly sea that was breaking 'solid' in tons on her decks. 'Why, she was just smothered in it sometimes, and every big sea was just a-flying all over her.' Her masts they saw were still standing, and her crew of seven were cowering for refuge between the main and mizzen masts under the weak shelter of the weather bulwarks, and also under the lee of the long boat, which still held its place, being firmly fastened to the deck. The fierce breakers burst rather over her quarter; had they swept quite broadside over her, the boat would have been torn from its fastenings long before.

As the Deal lifeboat stood in towards the Goodwins, they saw that their noble rivals the Ramsgate tug and lifeboat in tow had arrived on the scene a few minutes before them, and were close to the wreck.

The Ramsgate tug Aid now cast off the lifeboat, which got up sail and made in through the breakers with the wind right aft impelling her forwards at speed. The tug of course waited outside the surf, in deep water. The Deal men, separated from the Ramsgate lifeboat by about four hundred yards, were breathless spectators of the event. They watched her plunging and lifting into and over each sea and on towards the wreck.

The Ramsgate men could not lie or ride alongside the vessel to windward ; there was too terrible a sea on that side, and therefore, in spite of the danger of the masts falling, they were obliged to go to leeward, or to the sheltered side of the vessel.

Just as the Ramsgate lifeboat was coming under the stern of the wreck and about to haul down foresail and shoot up alongside her, she was struck by a terrific sea. The Deal men saw this and shouted 'She's capsized !' The Ramsgate lifeboat was indeed almost, but not quite capsized, and she was also shot forwards and caught under the cat-head and anchor of the wreck. The captain of the wrecked vessel told me afterwards that he thought she was lost, but it was happily not so, and the Ramsgate lifeboatmen anchored, after recovering themselves, ahead of the vessel and veered down to her.

But the tidal current which runs over the Goodwins varies in a very irregular manner according to the wind that is blowing, and, contrary to their calculations, swept the Ramsgate lifeboat to the full length of her cable away from the vessel.

They naturally expected to find the usual off-tide from the land before and at high-water, which would have carried them towards the vessel when they anchored under her lee ; but instead of that there was running a strong 'in-tide,' which swept them helplessly away from the vessel, and rendered them absolutely unable to reach her, though anchored only two hundred yards off.

The seamen on the wreck, in order to reach by some means the lifeboat which had thus been borne away from them so mysteriously, threw a fender, with line attached, overboard, hoping that it too would follow the current which carried away the lifeboat, and that thus communications would be established between them ; but the currents round the ship held the fender close to the wreck, and kept it eddying under her lee.

All eyes were now turned to the advancing Deal lifeboat battling in the thickest of the surf. Both the Ramsgate men with warm sympathy and the shipwrecked crew with keen anxiety watched the Deal men's attempt, as they raced into the wild breakers.

The poor fellows clinging to the masts feared lest the Deal lifeboat too might miss them, and that they might all be lost before either lifeboat could reach them again, and they beckoned the Deal men on.

The very crisis of their fate was at hand, but there were no applauding multitudes or shouts of encouragement, only the cold wastes and solitudes of wild tumbling breakers around the lifeboatmen on that grey

dawn, and only the appealing helpless crew in a little
cluster on the wreck.

It was now 4 a.m., and the Deal coxswain, cool and
sturdy as his native Kentish oak, knowing that the
combination of an easterly gale with neap tides sometimes produces an 'in-tide' at high-water, and seeing the
Ramsgate lifeboat carried to leeward, gave the order
to 'down foresail!' when well outside the wreck, and
anchored E. by S. of her. Thus the same 'in-tide'

which swept the Ramsgate lifeboat away from the
wreck, carried the Deal lifeboat right down to her.

It will be remembered that the head of the Golden
Island lay N.W., and the accompanying diagram will
enable the reader to understand that as the lifeboat
anchored in nearly the opposite quarter, viz. about S.E.,
her head, as she ranged alongside the wreck, lay in
precisely the opposite direction to the head of the shipwrecked schooner.

The Deal lifeboat coxswain now hoisted a bit of his foresail to sheer her in towards the wreck, but from the position of his anchor he could not get closer than ten fathoms, or twenty yards.

To bridge this gulf of boiling surf, the cane loaded with lead, to which a light line was attached, had to be hurled by a stalwart arm, and John May succeeded in throwing the 'lead line' on board the wreck.

As the half-drowned and perishing crew of the wreck saw the Deal lifeboat winning her way towards them, and inch by inch conquering the opposing elements, their hearts revived.

They saw within hailing distance of them—for their cries could be heard plainly enough coming down the wind by the Deal men—the brave, determined faces of their rescuers, and they felt that God had not forsaken them, but had wrought for them a great deliverance.

Having gone through all that surf, and having got within reach as it were of the wreck, the crew of the Deal lifeboat were now eager for the final rescue. They never speak of, or even allude to the feeling on such occasions within them, yet we know their hearts were on fire for the rescue, and men in that mood are not easily to be baulked or to be beaten.

As the wearied seamen grasped the meaning of the Deal coxswain's shouts, or rather signs, for shouts against the wind were almost inaudible, they aided in rigging up veering and hauling lines, by which they would have to be dragged through the belt of surf which lay between them and the lifeboat.

A clove-hitch, which my readers can practise for themselves, was passed round the waist of the captain's son, a boy of thirteen, who was first to leave the wreck.

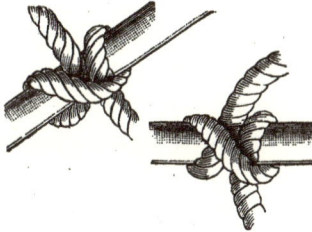

CLOVE-HITCH.

The lad naturally enough shrank from facing the boiling caldron which raged between him and the lifeboat, and with loud cries clung to his father. Waiting was impossible, and he had to be separated partly by persuasion and partly by main force from his father's arms and dragged through the sea. When once he was in the water the boatmen pulled at him with all their might, and when alongside, two strong men reached over the side and hoisted him like a feather into the lifeboat.

The men said 'he cried dreadful,' and the coxswain found a moment to tell him, ' Don't cry, my little fellow ! we'll soon have your father into the lifeboat.' But with the words came a sea 'that smothered us all up, and it wanted good holding to keep ourselves from being carried overboard.' Some kind-hearted fellows, till the sea passed, held the boy, but still he kept crying, ' Come, father ! Come, father ! '

Three more of the crew then got the 'clove-hitch ' over their shoulders and jumped into the sea ; some of them helped themselves by swimming and kept their heads up; others merely gripped the rope and fared much worse, being pulled head under, but all three were quickly dragged through the water into the lifeboat.

I have said dragged through the 'water'; but surf is not the same as water—it is water lashed into froth or seething bubbles in mountainous masses. You can swim in water; but the best swimmer sinks in 'froth,' and can only manage and spare himself till the genuine water gives him a heave up and enables him to continue the struggle on the surface.

Now water that breaks into surf is not merely motionless 'froth,' that is half air and half water, but it runs at speed, and being partly composed of solid water strikes any obstacle with enormous force and smashes like a hammer. These then were the characteristics of the sea which beat all round the wreck, and through which the half-dazed and storm-beaten sailors had to be dragged.

Besides the veering and hauling line by which the sailors in distress came, there was another line passed round the mast of the tossing lifeboat, to hold her in spite of her plunging as close as possible to the ship; and this line had to be eased with each sea and then the slack hauled in again. Some better idea will be given of the nature of this deadly wrestle, when I mention that this line cut so deeply into the mast as to render it unsafe, and it was never again used after that day.

The sails of the wrecked vessel were clattering and blowing about, 'like kites '—indeed, they were in ribbons; and the wind in the rigging was like the harsh roar of an approaching train, so that in the midst of this wild hurly-burly even the men in the lifeboat could hardly hear each other's shouts.

Roberts now saw that it was necessary to shift the cable as it lay on the bow of the lifeboat, and he shouted to his comrades forward to have this done; but 'the wind was a blowin' and the sea a 'owling that dreadful' that not a man could hear what he said, and he sprang forward to shift the cable himself. That very moment round the stern of the wreck there swept the huge green curl of a gigantic sea, which, just as it reached the lifeboat, broke with a roar a ton of water into her.

It took Roberts off his feet, so that he must have gone overboard, but for the foremast against which it dashed him, and to which he clung desperately, as the great wave melted away hissing, to leeward. Shaking off the spray, the drenched lifeboatmen again turned to the work of rescue; the coxswain having been preserved by his thick cork lifebelt from what might otherwise have been a fatal crush.

This weighty sea tore away the lines and all means of communication between the wreck and the lifeboat, and drove the three remaining sailors on the vessel away from the shelter of the long boat to the bows of the wreck. Indeed, as they grasped for dear life the belaying pins on the foremast, the sea covered them up to their shoulders, and they were all but carried away.

Again the loaded cane had to be thrown; again the task was entrusted to John May, who sent it flying through the air, and again the veering and hauling line was rigged, and the remaining seamen were got into the lifeboat.

I

The last man has to see to it for his life that the veering line is clear, and that it is absolutely free from anything that could catch or jam it or prevent it running out freely.

Just as coming down a steep ice slope where steps have to be cut by men roped together, the best man should come last, so the last man rescued from a wreck should have a good clear head and the stoutest heart of all; and last man came bravely the captain, to the great joy of his little son.

Then the lifeboatmen turned to preparations for home. They dared not get in their cable and heave their anchor on board, lest they should be carried back and dashed against the wreck, the danger of which, a glance at the sketch will show. So they got a spring on the cable, to cant the lifeboat's head to starboard or landsward, and with a parting 'Hurrah!' they slipped their cable, of course thus sacrificing it and their anchor. They hoisted their foresail, and with a gale of wind behind them raced into and through the surf on the Goodwins, which lay between them and home.

The Goodwins are four miles wide, and the land was eight miles distant, but a splendid success had crowned the brave and steadfast Deal coxswain's efforts. Not a man was lost, and they had with them in the lifeboat the shipwrecked vessel's crew—all saved.

It was a noble sight to see the lifeboat nearing the land that morning at 7 a.m. The British red ensign was flying proudly from her peak, in token of 'rescued crew on board'; and as the men jumped out, I grasped the brave coxswain's hand and said, 'Well done, Roberts!' And as I saw the rescued crew and their gallant deliverers, 'God bless you, my lads, well done!' The words will be echoed in many a heart, but could my readers have seen the faces of the lifeboatmen, weather-beaten and incrusted with salt, or watched them, as they staggered wearied but rejoicing up the beach—could they have knelt in the thanksgiving service which I held that morning with the rescued crew, and have heard their graphic version of the grim reality—and how that the living God had in His mercy stretched out His arm and saved them from death on the Goodwins, they would better understand,—better, far, than words of mine can bring it home—how splendid a deed of mercy and of daring was that day done by the coxswain and the crew of the North Deal lifeboat[1].

[1] The names of the crew of the lifeboat on this occasion (being one man short, which was not observed in the darkness of the launch) were—Richd. Roberts (coxswain), G. Marlowe, John May, Henry May, Wm. Hanger, Ed. Pain, R. Betts, G. Brown, David Foster, Wm. Nicholas, Henry Roberts, R. Ashington, John Adams, John Marsh.

CHAPTER VIII

THE SORRENTO, S.S.

And the clamorous bell spake out right well
To the hamlet under the hill,
And it roused the slumb'ring fishers, nor its warning task gave o'er,
Till a hundred fleet and eager feet were hurrying to the shore.

THAT Norse and Viking blood is to be found in the E. and S.E. coasts of England is tolerably certain. Tradition, as well as the physical characteristics of the people. go to support the belief that the inhabitants of the little picturesque village of Kingsdown, midway on the coast line between Deal and the South Foreland, are genuine 'Sons of the Vikings.'

Kingsdown looks seaward, just facing the southern end of the Goodwin Sands, and at the back of the pretty village, which is built on the shingle of the beach, rise the chalk cliffs which culminate in the South Foreland, a few miles farther on. Here in days gone by the samphire gatherer plied his 'dreadful trade,' and still from the wooded cliff 'the fishermen that walk upon the beach appear like mice.'

Like their Deal brethren, the hardy boatmen of Kingsdown live by piloting and fishing, and, like the Deal

JARVIST ARNOLD.

men, have much to do with the Goodwin Sands. The
same may be said of the more numerous Walmer boatmen ; and all three are usually summed up in the general
and honourable appellation of Deal boatmen.

The Kingsdown villagers are believed to be Jutes,

and the names prevalent amongst them add probability
to the idea. Certainly there is a Norse flavour about
the name of Jarvist Arnold, for many years coxswain of
the Kingsdown lifeboat Sabrina. This brave, fine old
seaman still survives, and still his eye kindles, and his

voice still rings, as with outstretched hand and fire un-
quenched by age he tells of grapples with death on the
Goodwin Sands. He is no longer, alas! equal to the
arduous post which he nobly held for twenty years, a
post now well filled by James Laming, Jarvist's comrade
in many a risky job; but still he is regarded with rever-
ence and affection, and the rescue of the crew of the
Sorrento and the story of the 'old cork fender' will
always be honourably associated with his name. Round
him the incidents of this chapter will group themselves,
for, though brave men were his crew on each occasion,
he was the guiding spirit.

The mode of manning the Kingsdown lifeboat is
somewhat different from the practice of Deal and
Walmer, as will be seen, but in all three cases the same
rush of eager men is made to gain the honourable post
of a place in the lifeboat.

Sometimes the launch is utterly unavailing, as was the
case on a December night in 1867, when with Jarvist
Arnold at the helm, the lifeboat sped into and through
the tossing surf and 'fearful sea' (the coxswain's words),
across the south end of the Goodwins, and found a barque
from Sunderland on fire and drifting on to the sands.
So hot it was from the flames that they could not if they
would go to leeward of her, and they kept to windward,
witnessing the spectacle of a ship on fire in a midnight
'hurricane from the west.' There was no one on board
of the burning ship, and no one knows the fate of her
crew. Sadly the lifeboatmen returned to the land.

Again Jarvist Arnold is summoned to the rescue, and
this time with a different result. On February 12, 1870,
all the vessels in the Downs were driven ashore, with the

From a Painting]

A SCENE ON DEAL BEACH, FEBRUARY 13, 1870.

[by W. H. Franklin.

exception of one, which the skill and pluck of E. Hanger, second coxswain of the Deal lifeboat, safely piloted away to safety, through the tremendous sea.

There was a great gale from E.S.E. with bitter cold and snow. Vessel after vessel came ashore, and some were torn into matchwood along the beach. One large vessel, the ship Glendura, having parted her anchors in the great sea that was running, was driving landwards. The captain, foreseeing the inevitable, and determined, if he could not save his vessel, to save precious lives—his wife and child being on board—boldly set his lower foretopsail, to force his vessel stem on as far ashore on the mainland as possible ; and about 9 p.m., in this dark freezing snowstorm, the stem of his large vessel, drawing about twenty-three feet of water, struck the land.

The engraving shows this ship in the act of striking. Facing the picture, the Glendura lies farthest from the spectator. Between her and the land would be about 100 fathoms, or 200 yards of water ; but that water was one furious mass of advancing billows hurled landwards by this great tempest.

Fortunately, as I have said, the Glendura struck the beach unlike the other vessels in the engraving, not broadside on, but stem on. They were broken up very soon ; but the Glendura held together, burning flares and sending up appealing rockets. Still more fortunately— but in truth providentially is the word to use—she struck right opposite Kingsdown lifeboat house, where lay head to storm-blast, the Kingsdown lifeboat Sabrina, and where, grouped round her, Jarvist Arnold and the lifeboat crew stood ready.

Had the wrecked ship come ashore at any distance

from the spot where the lifeboat lay, either to the right or left, that is, either west or east of where she did strike, the probability is that all on board would have perished. With a heavy gale dead on shore, if the lifeboat had succeeded in launching, she would not have fetched the wreck, had she lain any distance either side, but would have been helplessly beaten back again.

The Kingsdown men were keenly watching the approaching catastrophe as the Glendura came landwards. Long before she struck, the little fishing village echoed to the cry of ' Man the lifeboat,' and clad in their sou'-westers and lifebelts the brave crew waited for the crash of the doomed vessel, which, by God's mercy, took place right in front of them. The sea they had to face was terrific, and so bitter was the night that the sea spray froze as it was borne landwards by the blast, and each rope in the ship's rigging was thick with ice.

Just as the men were all in the lifeboat, and were about to man their haul-off warp to pull the lifeboat out into deep water thereby, a service of the greatest danger on such a night, some one on the beach—it was James Laming, the present able Kingsdown coxswain, but then a very young man—even in that black night discovered a great fender floating in the recoil. It was pulled ashore, and it was then found that a line was attached to it, and to that line a weightier one ; and to that a four and a-half inch hawser, or strong cable, leading from the wrecked ship to the land.

Perceiving the object of those on board, Jarvist Arnold gave the order to ' Let the lifeboat go,' and she plunged down the steep beach into the black billows of that easterly snowstorm and right into the very teeth of it.

No sooner had they touched the water than they hauled upon the cable which had been sent ashore from the vessel ; and so, bit by bit, one moment submerged and the next swung on the crest of some stormy wave, they gradually hauled themselves out to the vessel, and found the crew with the captain and his wife and child gathered in a forlorn little cluster out on the jib-boom.

Right under the martingale with its sharp spear-like head the lifeboat had to lie. When a monstrous sea came roaring round the stern of the vessel, the lifeboat had to let go and come astern, lest she should be impaled on the sharp point, as she was hoisted up with great force.

Back again the crew hauled her, and when the furious sea had passed, in answer to shouts of 'Come on!' 'Now's your time!' down a rope into the lifeboat came the second mate with the captain's child in his arms. Up the stiff half-frozen rope again he climbed and brought down the captain's wife ; and some more of the crew rapidly came the same way. Then the lifeboat having their full complement of people on board, some of whom were perishing with the cold of that awful night, made for the land ; still holding the cable from the ship they drifted, or rather were hurled ashore, in the darkness, pelted by hail and snow and drenched by the seas, which broke with force clean over them.

The task of landing the enfeebled crew and the poor lady and child in such a great sea was dangerous, but it was accomplished safely. Indeed, such was the sympathy and enthusiasm of the Kingsdown villagers and fisher-folk that, if need were, they could and would have carried the lifeboat with its human freight right up the beach.

An attempt was now made to use the rocket apparatus, and a rocket was fired, which went clean through the fore-topsail and to the poop of the vessel behind. Another whizzing rocket, carrying its line with it, went hurtling through or close to the crowd clustered on the top-gallant forecastle, where they cowered before creeping out on to the bowsprit. No harm was done by the erratic flight of the rockets, but the wrecked sailors naturally preferred to go ashore in the lifeboat to being dragged through the breakers in the cradle of the rocket-apparatus, and declining to use it, they again summoned the lifeboat.

The first crew of the lifeboat were worn out with their exertions, and the blows and buffetings of the freezing sea-spray. A fresh crew was therefore obtained, all but the coxswain, Jarvist Arnold, who stuck to his post. Back again to the ship the lifeboatmen hauled themselves, through such a sea that words which would truly describe it must seem exaggerated. Remember the bows of the ship lay nearly two hundred yards from the land in a veritable cauldron of waters.

Again the lifeboat returned with her living freight of rescued seamen, and again worn out as before with the struggle, a fresh crew was obtained; but again Jarvist Arnold for the third time went back to the wreck. And yet again with a fourth fresh crew the brave man returned for the fourth and last time to the vessel; and finally came safe to the shore with the remainder of the crew, twenty-nine of whom were thus rescued, but only rescued by the most determined and repeated efforts, through what the coxswain's report describes as 'a fearful sea with snowstorm and freezing hard all the time.'

When, long after midnight, the lifeboatmen staggered home, Jarvist found that his oilskin coat was frozen so hard that it stood upright and rigid on his cottage floor when he took it off his own half-frozen self. But he had a soft pillow that night ; he had bravely done his duty, and had saved twenty-nine of his fellow human beings from death in the sea.

Many a stormy struggle after this rescue was gone through by Jarvist Arnold and his Kingsdown lifeboat crew on the Goodwin Sands during the years 1870–1872. Holding the honourable but arduous post of coxswain of the Kingsdown lifeboat Sabrina, he also manfully earned his living as Channel pilot, being a most trustworthy and skilful seaman. He did well that which came to his hand; he did his best and his duty. I speak after the manner of men, and as between man and man. More than that no man can do.

On the night of December 17, 1872, about 2.30 a.m., it was blowing a gale from the south-west. Out of the gale was borne landwards the boom of guns ; far away on the horizon, or where the horizon ought to be, was seen the flash of their fire ; and upwards into the winter midnight shot the distant rockets, appealing not in vain for help.

Almost simultaneously the coxswains at Walmer and Kingsdown were roused, William Bushell and Jarvist Arnold. At Walmer the lifeboat-bell rang out its summons, but at Kingsdown a fast runner was sent round the village, crying as he ran, 'Man the lifeboat!' 'Ship on the Goodwins!' Up sprang the men—that is, all the grown-up men in the village ; and while the tempest shook their lowly cottage roofs, out they poured into the night, followed by lads, boys, wives, mothers, sweethearts and sisters.

Jarvist Arnold's wife said, 'Ladies can sometimes keep their husbands, but poor women like us must let them go ;' and once more Jarvist Arnold steered his lifeboat—shall I not say to victory? for 'Peace hath her victories no less renowned than War ;' and this sentence might well be emblazoned on every lifeboat in the kingdom.

At 3 a.m. on this midwinter night they launched at their respective stations, distant about two miles from each other, the lifeboats of Walmer and Kingsdown, and faced the sea and the storm. Think of the deed, and its hardships, and its heroism; of the brave hearts who 'darkling faced the billows,' and the anxious women left behind, ye who live to kill time in graceless self-indulgence, and ere it be too late, learn to sacrifice and to dare.

The two lifeboats got together before they reached the edge of the Goodwins, and held such consultation as was possible in the pitchy darkness and in the roar of the sea. It was agreed between them that there would be much difficulty in finding the vessel in distress, as her signals and blue lights had ceased and the night was very dark. They decided that the Kingsdown lifeboat should go first, and if they hit the vessel they were to burn a red light in token of success, and a white light if they could not find her ; but that, in any case, Walmer was to come shortly after them and search through the breakers, whether Kingsdown succeeded or not.

In the dark the Kingsdown coxswain put his lifeboat into the surf on the Goodwins; it was heavy, but they got through it safely, and found on the off-part of the

Goodwins, towards its southern end—known as the South
Calliper—a large steamship aground. She proved to
be the Sorrento, bound from the Mediterranean to
Lynn.

Close outside where she lay on the treacherous sands
were thirteen and fourteen fathoms of deep water, that
is, from seventy to eighty feet, while she lay in about
six feet of white surf, which flew in clouds over her as
each sea struck her quarters and stern.

The Sorrento had struck the Goodwins at midnight,
or a little after, in about twenty-one feet of water, but
when the lifeboat got alongside the tide had fallen, and
there was only six feet of broken water around her. As
the sands were nearly dry to the southward of her, the
sea was by no means so formidable as it afterwards became with the rising tide and increasing gale and greater
depth of water.

The Kingsdown lifeboat sent up her red light, and
then came through the surf the Walmer lifeboat, guided
by the red signal of success from Jarvist Arnold. Both
lifeboats got alongside the great steamer, and the greater
part of the crews of both lifeboats clambered on board
her, leaving eight men in each lifeboat.

The head of the wrecked steamer lay about E.N.E.,
and the seas were hammering at and breaking against
her starboard quarter, which rose high in the air quite
twenty feet out of the water at the time the lifeboats got
alongside. All the lifeboatmen now turned to pumping
the vessel, which was very full of water, with a view to
saving the ship and her valuable cargo of barley.

The Walmer lifeboat lay alongside the Sorrento, under
her port bow, and the head of the Walmer lifeboat

pointed towards the stern of the wrecked steamer, and
was firmly fastened to her by a stout hawser.

About this time—say, five o'clock in the morning—
while it was dark, the Ramsgate lifeboat also arrived,
and seeing the other two lifeboats alongside they
anchored outside the sands. And the Kingsdown lifeboat, manned only by her coxswain and seven of her
crew, was sheered off about two hundred fathoms, to
lay out a kedge anchor, with a view to preventing the
vessel drifting farther, as the tide rose, into the shallower
parts of the sands, and in the hope of warping her into
deeper water.

Naturally the presence of the lifeboats and a company of seventeen or eighteen stalwart lifeboatmen, all
thoroughly up to their work, infused fresh courage into
the captain and crew of the Sorrento. They felt that all
was not lost, and dividing themselves into different
gangs of men, all hands worked with a will, throwing
the cargo overboard to lighten the vessel, and pumping
with all their energies—their shouts ringing out bravely
as they worked to get out the water. The donkey
engine too was set at work, and steam fought storm
and sea, but this time in vain. After several hours'
hard work, the engineer came to the captain and lifeboatmen and said, 'It's all up; the water's coming in
as fast as we pump it out. Come down and see for
yourselves!'

It was too true, the good steamship's back was broken,
and the clear sea-water bubbled into her faster than it
could be got out. As the day began to break, the sea
rose and beat more heavily over the vessel; it burst no
longer merely in clouds or showers on the deck, but in

heavy volumes, and on all sides, especially to the south; long lines of rollers careered on towards the doomed vessel with tossing, tumbling crests, and then burst over her.

At 11 a.m. in this state of affairs the hope of saving the ship was abandoned, and all only thought now of saving life. Thinking the two lifeboats—the Centurion and the Sabrina—were insufficient to rescue the whole of the steamer's crew, the ensign was hoisted 'union down' for more assistance. None came; probably the signal was not seen, or possibly, it was thought that the presence of the lifeboats had answered the appeal.

As the tide rose the water deepened and more wind came. Heavy masses of water struck the hapless vessel, and though her starboard quarter was still ten feet out of the water, each sea swept her decks, carrying spars, hen coops, and everything movable clean before it.

All hands now fled to the bridge of the steamer, watching for a favourable moment to get into the Walmer lifeboat, still riding alongside, while each mad billow lifted her up almost to the level of the bridge and then smothered the lifeboat in its foaming bosom as she descended into the depths.

Any one who carefully observes a succession of waves either breaking in charging lines on a beach, or in the wilder turmoil of the Goodwins, must notice how frequently they differ in shape and in size. I am by no means convinced that either the third wave—the τρικυμία of the Greeks—or the tenth wave, as the Latin *fluctus decimanus* seems to suggest—is always larger than its

K 2

tempestuous comrades, but ashore or afloat you do now and then see a giant, formed mysteriously in accordance with the laws of fluids, that does out-top its fellows, κεφαλήν τε καὶ εὔρεας ὤμους.

Such a great sea was seen advancing by the occupants of the bridge of the Sorrento. Combing, curling, high over the stern of the wreck it broke, carrying everything before it in one common ruin. It carried away the boats of the wrecked steamer, tearing them and the davits which supported them out of the vessel.

Snap went the strong five-inch cable which fastened the Walmer lifeboat to the port or sheltered quarter of the Sorrento, as the end of the great green sea swept round her stern ; and as the lifeboat was torn away from the wreck she was forced up against the crashing jangle of the steamer's boats and davits ; and yet again with tremendous force jammed right up against the anchor of the Sorrento, which was driven into the fore thwart of the ascending lifeboat. The lifeboatmen crouched down to avoid destruction, and—for all this was done in a moment—away she sped, spun round as a boy would spin his top, to leeward of the wreck and among the breakers of the Goodwins.

'Never saw anything spin round like her in my life!' said one of the crew afterwards ; and so far was she carried by this great sea that she could not drop anchor till she was half a mile from the wrecked steamship. Tide and wind were both against her, and she was utterly unable to get back to the wreck. She simply rode helplessly to her anchor with less than half of her own men in her, the remainder being clustered on the bridge, as already described, or clinging to the rigging of the Sorrento. The aspect of affairs had now become one of extreme gravity.

The Walmer lifeboat was swept away, and as helpless as if she were fifty miles off, leaving seven of her crew in great peril on the bridge. Seven of the crew of the Kingsdown lifeboat were also gathered on the steamer's bridge, together with thirty-two of the crew of the wrecked vessel herself. In all, there stood or clung there, drenched by the clouds of spray, drowned almost as they fought for breath, forty-six persons; and their only hope or chance for life was the Kingsdown lifeboat, which still bravely lived, heavily plunging into and covered now and then by the seas.

At the helm, in dire anxiety, was Jarvist Arnold, and with him were in the lifeboat only seven of his crew, the remainder of them being entrapped on board the Sorrento, together with the Walmer lifeboatmen. It was thought, as my readers will remember, that two lifeboats were insufficient to rescue all hands, but now the rescue—if rescue there were to be—depended upon one small lifeboat half manned.

Besides this, Jarvist Arnold saw with his own eyes the defeat of the Walmer lifeboat, and was so close to the wreck that he was well aware of the dangerous sea sweeping over her and racing up under her stern; but the brave fellow never faltered in his determination to attempt the rescue; and he was strung to his formidable task by the knowledge that three of his own sons were holding on for dear life on the bridge of the wreck. He could see the gestures and hear the shouts from the bridge as the sounds came across the wind, now a heavy gale.

There was no lack of resolution, but the problem was to get at the Sorrento at all, as the diagram will help the reader to understand.

It will be plain that the tide current was forcing the Kingsdown lifeboat, even when at anchor, away from the distressed vessel, and that if she weighed anchor, she would be carried away to leeward, as the Walmer men had been.

Thinking of all expedients, they bent on their second

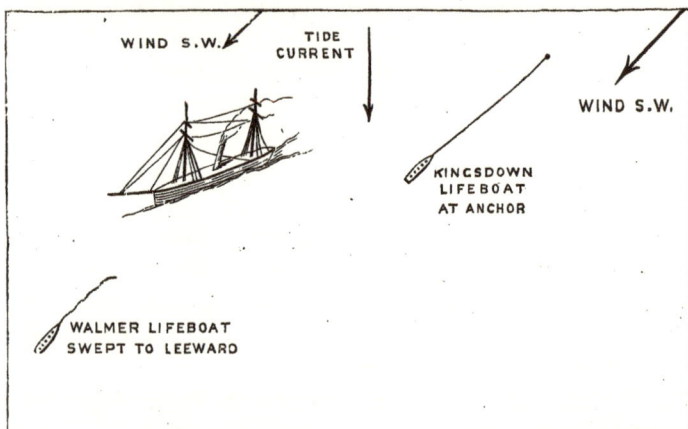

cable and rode to the long scope of one hundred and sixty fathoms. Still the cruel lee-tide and wind forced them away. They sheered the head of the lifeboat in towards the wreck—and then—the six men in her sprang to the oars, and tugged and strained at them, all rowing on the same side, to direct the lifeboat towards the vessel. While they struggled, the great breakers overwhelmed and blinded them, filling many times the gallant little lifeboat—she was only thirty-six feet in length—which

THE SORRENTO ON THE GOODWIN SANDS.

as obstinately emptied herself free and lived through it all, by God's good providence.

'Must I see my sons die in my sight, and my friends and neighbours too?' thought Jarvist Arnold, as he was beaten away from the vessel; and then, 'Lord, help me!' Again and again, in vain they struggled, when some one on the wreck sprang from the bridge at the most imminent peril of his life, on to the slippery, sloping wave-swept deck.

He had seen coiled on a belaying pin on the bridge a long lead line, and on the deck still unwashed away an old cork fender. Some say it was the mate of the vessel; others that it was one of the Kingsdown men who fastened the lead line to the fender and who slung it overboard, and then, stumbling and slipping, ran for his life back to the bridge, barely escaping an overwhelming wave.

Swirling and eddying in the strange currents on the Goodwins, and beaten of the winds and waves, on came the old cork fender towards the lifeboat. They had not another bit of cable to spare on board the lifeboat; every inch of their one hundred and sixty fathoms was paid out. Breathless the coxswain, and the man in the bows, rigid as his own boat-hook with the anxiety of the moment, lashed to his position, a life line round his waist, watched the approach of the fender. It was sucked by the current towards the lifeboat, and then tossed by a wave away from her again.

Feeling assured that a great loss of life must soon occur, either by the people on the frail refuge of the steamer's bridge being swept off it, or by the bridge itself being carried away by the seas, which were becoming more solid every moment, Jarvist and his comrades thought the cork fender was a long time in reaching them. Lives of men hung in the balance, and minutes seem hours then.

At last it drifted hopelessly out of reach, but into a curious backwater, which eddied it right under the boat hook of the bowman. In an instant it was seized, and the line made fast to a thwart. 'I've a great mind to trust to it,' said Jarvist Arnold, but caution prevailed, and they made fast a stout rope to the lead line.

Again the people on the bridge watched their chance. One man managed to wade along the now submerged deck to reach the lead line, and he hauled it with the stronger rope on board, making the latter securely fast. Again had this man to fly for life up the bridge from an advancing billow, which, leaping over the stern of the wreck, nearly overtook him, and at the same time by its great weight and impulse, beat the stern of the steamship a little way round to the west.

Hauling on this cable without letting go their own anchor, Jarvist Arnold and his small crew hauled their lifeboat as close under the leaning bridge as they dared.

The first man who tried to escape from the bridge in his leap missed the lifeboat and fell into the sea, and not a moment too soon was grasped by friendly hands and dragged into the lifeboat.

The direction of the tidal current on the Goodwins shifts every hour to a different point of the compass; and now this strong eddy, being altered still more by the position of the wreck, would suck the lifeboat towards the stern of the wreck. There she would meet another current of the truer tide, and get hurried back again half buried in breakers, which were ever and anon bursting over and round the stern of the wreck.

Then she would come back under the bridge, where every effort was made to hold her by stern ropes; and as she rose, 'by the dreadful tempest borne, high on the broken wave,' man after man they jumped, or were dragged, or came quick as lightning down a rope, into the Sabrina, the whole forty-six of the imperilled men, the captain being last man, and almost too late.

Bringing with them the old cork fender as a memento, Jarvist and his unbeaten crew sheered out their lifeboat to ride by their own cable, as before the timely arrival of the fender. Now they saw signs of the approaching break up of the Sorrento, for before they had left her very long her funnel and masts went overboard, and reeling to the blows of the sea, she split in halves and disappeared under the breakers of the Goodwins.

But before this dramatic conclusion, the Kingsdown lifeboat slipped her anchor, to which she never could have got back, and setting her mast and double-reefed storm-foresail, ran away before the wind through the 'heavy boiling surf' on the Goodwins. These are the coxswain's own written words, and I can only repeat they are below the grim reality.

With the forty-six rescued seafarers on board she was terribly low in the water, and was filled in and out from both sides at once by the seas as they broke. Only a lifeboat could have lived, but even she resembled a floating baulk of timber, which is covered and swept by the seas on the same level as itself. Holding on for life to thwarts and life-lines, they kept the lifeboat dead before the sea. They did not dare to luff her to the west or bear her away to the east. They dared not keep away to get to the Walmer lifeboat, nor in the other direction toward the mainland, about six miles off.

The slightest exposure of the broadside of the lifeboat would either have capsized her, or washed every soul out of her; onwards, therefore, dead before the wind and right on the top of and in the breakers of the Goodwins she flew her stormy flight for nearly four miles.

The Walmer lifeboat had got up anchor at the same time as the Kingsdown men; for as the Kingsdown overcrowded lifeboat ran past the Walmer lifeboat, which was waiting at anchor for them, they shouted to the Walmer men, 'Slip your cable, and come after us!'

This the Walmer lifeboat did, and now ventured to approach the Kingsdown lifeboat. Though handled with skill and caution, being light, she took a sea; and she came right on top of the gunwale of the Kingsdown lifeboat, smashing her oars, which were run out to steady her, like so many pipe-shanks, and crunching into her gunwale.

But at last, with difficulty, half of the living freight of the Sabrina was transferred to the Walmer lifeboat; and then both lifeboats luffing in through Trinity Swatch, by God's mercy, escaped the deadly Goodwins, and landed the rescued crew at Broadstairs.

And the gallant deed is still sung by the Kingsdown children in simple village rhymes.

> God bless the Lifeboat and its crew,
> Its coxswain stout and bold,
> And Jarvist Arnold is his name,
> Sprung from the Vikings old,

Who made the waves and winds their slaves,
  As likewise we do so,
While still Britannia rules the waves,
  And the stormy winds do blow;
And the old Cork Float that safety brought,
  We'll hold in honour leal,
And it shall grace the chiefest place
  In Kingsdown, hard by Deal!

One of Jarvist Arnold's sons never recovered the strain of those awful hours on the bridge of the Sorrento in her death-throes, and, to use his father's words : ' He never was a man no more.' But Jarvist himself did many a subsequent good deed of rescue, and stuck to his arduous post as long as, and even beyond, what health and strength and age permitted.

Would that I could say that the noble old fellow was in independent circumstances ! Despite the continued generosity of the Royal National Lifeboat Institution to him, alas! this is not the case. Would that some practicable scheme for providing a pension for deserving working men in their old age were before the country !

Jarvist Arnold is, however, not forsaken ; he has good and honourable children, and I know·that with that inner gaze which sees more clearly as eternity approaches, he too in simple faith beholds the advancing lifeboat, and hears the glad words, ' When thou passest through the waters, I will be with thee ; and through the rivers, they shall not overflow thee,' from the mouth of the Great Commander.

CHAPTER IX

THE ROYAL ARCH

Cease, rude Boreas, blust'ring railer!
List, ye landsmen all, to me!
Messmates! hear a brother sailor
Sing the dangers of the sea.

THIS and the following chapter contains the story of cases of rescue in which the ships in distress were saved, together with all on board, by the skill and courage of the Deal lifeboatmen, and brought finally with their respective cargoes safe into port.

A century ago, certain of our English coasts are described by the same writer whose lines head this chapter, as—

Where the grim hell-hounds, prowling round the shore,
With foul intent the stranded bark explore.
Deaf to the voice of woe, her decks they board,
While tardy Justice slumbers o'er her sword.

But these pages recount, in happy contrast, the generous and gallant efforts of the Deal boatmen, in the first instance to save life, and then, when besought to stand by the vessel, or employed to do so, of their further success in saving valuable property, often worth many thousand pounds, from utter destruction in the sea.

I stood some years ago on the deck of a lightship stationed near the wreck of the British Navy, a vessel sunk by collision in the Downs one dreadful night, when twenty sailors went to the bottom with her, and I saw her masts blown up and out of her by an explosion of dynamite to remove the wreck from the Downs, while the water was strewn with the débris of her valuable cargo. This cargo, amongst countless other commodities, was said to have contained one hundred pianos; hence some idea may be gathered of the pecuniary importance, apart from the story's thrilling interest, of salvage of valuable vessels and precious merchandize.

On March 29, 1878, the wind blew strong from the E.N.E., and only one vessel, the Royal Arch, lay in the Downs. The great roadstead, protected from the full fetch of an easterly sea by the natural breakwater of the Goodwins—for without those dreaded sands neither the Downs as a sheltered anchorage would exist, nor in all probability the towns of Deal and Walmer—was nevertheless on that day a very stormy place, and as the wind freshened towards evening, as the east wind nearly always does in this locality, it eventually came on to blow a whole gale dead on shore.

The sea raised by an easterly gale on Deal beach is tremendous, and not even the first-class luggers, or their smaller sisters, the 'cats,' could be launched. Had there been a harbour from which the Deal luggers could at once make the open sea, they would have been able to live and skim like the stormy petrel over

the crest of the billows ; but it is quite a different thing
when a lugger has to be launched from a beach right in
the teeth of a mountainous sea, and incurs the certainty
of being driven back broadside on to the steep shingle,
and of her crew being washed out of her, and drowned
by some giant sea. Hence that evening no ordinary
Deal boat or even lugger could launch. On the morning
of the same day the captain of the Royal Arch had
been compelled by some necessary business to come
ashore. To have come ashore in his own ship's boat
in such a wind and sea would have involved certain
disaster and even loss of life, and therefore he came
ashore in a Deal galley punt, which successfully performed
the feat of beaching in a heavy surf.

In the evening, against an increasing gale, and much
heavier sea, the galley punt dared not launch to bring
the captain back. None even of the luggers would
encounter the risk of launching in so heavy a sea dead
on the beach. He therefore tried the lifeboats, upon
the plea and grounds that his ship was dragging her
anchors and in peril. She was lying abreast of Walmer
Castle, and was indeed gradually dragging in towards
the surf-beaten shore, which, if she struck, not a soul
on board probably would have been saved.

The anxious captain first tried the Walmer lifeboat,
but she was too far to leeward, and would not have
been able to fetch the vessel. But eventually, as his
vessel was now burning signals of distress, he ran to
the North Deal lifeboat, and the coxswain, Robert
Wilds, seeing all other boats were helpless, decided to
ring the lifeboat bell and pit the celebrated Van Cook
against the stormy sea in deadly fight.

The Deal boatmen had long foreseen the launch of the lifeboat, and they were massed in crowds round the lifeboat-house, competitors for the honour of forming the crew. The danger of the distressed vessel was known in the town, and crowds had assembled on the beach, amongst them the Mayor of Deal, to watch the lifeboat launch.

The long run of the great waves came right up to where the lifeboat lay, so that when she was let go she had no steep slope to rush down so as to hurl her by her own impetus into the sea. She depended, therefore, for her launching against this great sea, on her haul-off warp, which was moored one hundred fathoms out to sea, and by which her fifteen men hoped to pull her out to deep water. But this dark night she simply stuck fast after running down a little way, and got into the 'draw back' under the seas bursting in fury.

Her situation was most perilous, and the danger of the men being swept out of her was great. But through it all the lifeboatmen, with stubborn pluck, held on to the haul-off warp and strained for their lives, and at last a great sea came and washed them afloat within its recoil, and covered the lifeboat and her crew. The spectators groaned with horror as the lifeboat disappeared, but the men were straining gallantly at the haul-off warp, and the lifeboat emerged. When she was seen above the surges just only for an instant, ' All Deal sent forth a rapturous cry,' and the brave men, though they could not see the people on the land, yet heard their mighty cheer, and, strung in their hearts to dare and to conquer, sped on their glorious task.

L

When just out to deep water, the coxswain sang out, ' Hang on, every man ! ' and a great sea came out of the night right at the lifeboat. Tom Adams was out on the fore air-box, lifting the haul-off warp out of the cheek, a perilous spot, when the sea was seen ; he had just time to get back and clasp both arms round the foremast as the sea broke, overwhelming lifeboat and the crew and the captain of the Royal Arch, who was aft, in a white smother of foam. But the lifeboat freed herself of the sea, and like a living creature stood up to face the gale.

Close-reefed mizzen and reefed storm foresail was her canvas; watchful men stood by halyards and sheets, hitched, not belayed, and watched each gust and sea as only Deal men who watch for their lives can watch, and even they are sometimes caught.

At last the vessel in distress loomed through the night, and from many an anxious heart on board went up, ' Thank God! here comes the lifeboat ! ' Not too soon was she ! For the hungry breakers were roaring under their lee. Blue lights and other signals of distress had already been made on board the vessel for some time ; a rocket too had been fired, with a rather unsatisfactory result.

One of the mates, who I was informed hailed from County Cork, decided to fire a rocket, a thing he had never, it seems, done before in his life, and failing the usual rocket-stand, he bethought him of the novel and ingenious expedient of letting it off through the iron tube which formed the chimney of the galley or cooking-house on deck, thus hoping to make sure of successfully directing its flight upwards. In the confusion and darkness he did in his execution not perhaps do justice to himself, or to the fertility of resource which had devised so excellent a plan. The sea was rolling to the depth of two feet over the deck, and washing right through the galley house, and it was only by great efforts he succeeded in the darkness in fastening the rocket in the tube which formed the chimney.

To do this he had unwisely removed the rocket from its stick, and, unfortunately, he fastened it in the chimney upside down. Having done so, he fumbled in his pocket, the darkness being intense, for his matches, and applied the light underneath in the usual place. But the rocket being upside down he of course failed to set it off, and then he unluckily tried the other end, which was uppermost, with the disastrous result, as my English informant described it, that 'the hexplosion blowed him clean out of the galley.'

'Blowed him!' said I, unconsciously adopting my friend's expression, 'where?'

'Why,' said he, 'hout of the galley into the lee scuppers.'

'Was the poor fellow much hurt?'

'Hurt! Bless you! not he. But he kept shouting like forty blue murders!'

'What did he say?'

'Well,' he replied, 'he was that scared and that choked with soot, as ever was, that all he could say was—I'm dead! I'm dead! I'm dead!'

The position of the vessel was now very serious; she was going so fast astern towards the breakers and the land that after the lifeboat anchored ahead of and close to her she could hardly keep abreast of the dragging vessel by paying out her cable as fast as possible. Roberts and Adams, and in all five of the lifeboatmen, sprang on board of her as she rolled in the pitchy night.

They sprang, as the lifeboat went up and the ship came down, over the yawning chasm, on the chance of gripping the shrouds, and some of them rolled over and actually and literally, as they were carried off their feet, had to swim on the decks of the labouring vessel.

The captain of the vessel could not get on board in the same way, and though they passed a line round his waist it was a good half-hour before they could get him up the steep side.

The lifeboatmen say that when he did reach the deck he declared ' that if that was what they called coming hoff in a lifeboat from Deal beach, he wouldn't do it again—no, not for hall the money in the Bank of England !'

The captain now hesitated to slip his ship, lest she might pay off on the wrong tack and come ashore ; but as the vessel was steadily drifting and the sea terrific, the lifeboat being now and then hoisted up to her fore-yard, while mountainous seas wallowed over both the lifeboat and the vessel, the Deal lifeboatmen said, ' If you don't slip her, we will.   There's death right astern for all of us if you delay.'

Then the captain himself took the helm, the rudder-head being twisted, and the spirit and energy of the Deal men infused new life into the wearied crew, and all hands worked together with a will.

They loosed the fore-topsail and they set the fore-topmast staysail. Tom Adams went or waded forwards, holding on carefully, with a lantern, and he watched by the dim light till the fore-topmast staysail bellied out with a flap like thunder on the right side, and then he shouted down the wind, 'Hard up, captain! Hard a-port!' At the same instant Roberts shouted, 'Slip the cable! Let go all!' And just within the very jaws of the breakers, the ship's head payed away to the southward, and she escaped—saved at the last minute, and safe to the open sea.

When safe away and running before the gale, the Deal men strapped the rudder-head with ropes, straining them tight with a tackle, and then wedged the ropes tighter and tighter still, making the rudder head thoroughly safe.

And then, though only very poorly and miserably supplied with food—for they only had dry biscuits till they reached port—they manned the pumps with the worn-out crew, and brought the ship safe to Cowes.

But for the existence of a lifeboat at North Deal the ship would have been wrecked that night on the stormy beach of Deal, and, in all probability, her crew would also have perished.

It is pleasant to record the unselfish heroism of the Deal lifeboatmen, who on this occasion were the means of saving both valuable property and precious human lives.

CHAPTER X

THE MANDALAY

The leak we've found, it cannot pour fast ;
We've lightened her a foot or more—
Up and rig a jury foremast,
She rights ! She rights, boys ! Wear off shore !

THE case of the Mandalay here recorded so far
resembles that of the Royal Arch and of the Edina,
that in all three cases the vessels, the cargoes, and the
lives of all on board, were saved by the Deal lifeboatmen, and by their courage and seamanlike skill, and
intimate local knowledge of the Goodwins and other
places and sands in their dangerous vicinity, brought
safe to port. The Royal Arch was drifting at night
from her anchorage in the Downs, in an easterly gale
towards the surf-beaten shore. The Edina was in the
most imminent peril on the edge of the Brake Sand.
The Mandalay was on the Goodwins itself, and to save
a vessel and her cargo from the Goodwins is no easy
task.

On December 12, 1889, the Mandalay was passing
the North Sand Head lightship a little after midnight.

She was outward bound from Middlesbrough to the River Plate with a cargo of railway iron sleepers. They hailed the lightship as its great lantern rapidly flashed close to them, but the reply was lost in the plash of the sea and the flap of the sails and the different noises of a ship in motion. At any rate the Mandalay mistook her bearings, and managed to get into the very heart of the Goodwin Sands.

In the darkness she probably sailed into what is called the Ramsgate Man's Bight, though this is only a conjecture. This bight is a swatchway of deep water, and the Mandalay then struck the Sands on the eastern jaw of another channel into the Goodwins. This swatchway runs N.E. and S.W., and leads from the deep water outside the Goodwins into the inmost recesses of the Sands; that is, into a shallowish bay called Trinity Bay; and it is much harder to get out of this bay than to get in, like many a scrape of another kind. The swatchway leading into Trinity Bay was about seven fathoms deep, but only fifty fathoms or one hundred yards wide. On the eastern bank or jaw of this channel the Mandalay ran aground. She ran aground at nearly high water, when all was covered with the sea, on a fine, calm night, there being no surf or ripple or noise to indicate the shallow water or the deadly proximity of the Goodwin Sands.

Some of the crew were on deck—the man at the wheel aft would take a sight of the compass gleaming in the light of the binnacle lamp, and then cast his eye aloft, where the main truck was circling among the stars, as the ship gently swung along with a light N.W. breeze. Others of the crew were below and had turned in, 'their midnight fancies wrapped in golden dreams,' when the grating sound of contact with the Sands was heard.   Then came, 'Turn out, men! All hands on deck!   We're aground on the Good-wins!'

Efforts were made to box the ship off by backing and swinging the yards and trimming the sails, but all to no purpose, and then flares and torches to summon help were lighted.   These at once caught the notice of the look-out men on the lightships, and drew from those vessels the guns and rockets, the usual signals of distress.   As the sea was smooth there was no present danger for the Mandalay, but wind and sea rise suddenly on the Goodwins, and no one could foresee what might happen.

The Deal coxswain was roused by the coastguard; he saw the flash of the distant guns and rockets, and having obtained a crew launched at 1.30 a.m., the weather being hazy with frost.   They reached the Gull lightship, and heard there that the vessel ashore lay E.N.E. from them.   They steered in that direction, gazing into the darkness and listening for sounds or shouts or guns, and at last, about 3 a.m., found the vessel, her flares having gone out.   In spite of the efforts of those on board, she was sidling more and more on to the Sands, and settling further into them.

The lifeboat anchored and veered down as usual to the stranded vessel, and the coxswain got on board : then morning came, and with it low water, when there would be not more than two feet of water round the Mandalay and the lifeboat, which latter was at

that depth of water just aground. The lifeboat remained by the vessel, to insure the safety of the crew in
case of possible change of weather. About midday, as
the tide began to rise over the Goodwins, the lifeboat
and her crew were employed by the captain to do their
best to save the vessel.

The lifeboat was now on the port bow of the Mandalay, which lay fast on the Sands with her head to the
S.W., and the coxswains laid out a kedge or small
anchor, with warp attached, to the N.E., five of the
lifeboatmen remaining in the lifeboat with Roberts, the
coxswain, to direct the course of action on the Sands,
while Hanger, the second coxswain, went on board with
seven lifeboatmen to direct operations there, and to
heave on the warp, in order to move the vessel. Just
then a tug-boat hove in sight, and as the sea was calm,
she backed in and made fast her hawser to the Mandalay, at the captain's desire. Though all on board
heaved their best on the warp, and the tug-boat
Bantam Cock made every effort, they were unable
to move the Mandalay from her perilous position, and
the tug-boat then gave the matter up as a bad job and
later in the evening went away.

It was now about 3 p.m., and the tide was again
falling when the lugger Champion, of Ramsgate, appeared and anchored in the swatchway spoken of above.
Some of her crew also went on board the Mandalay,
and under the directions and advice of Roberts and
Hanger, the two Deal coxswains, who were determined
to win, all hands turned to throwing overboard the
cargo to lighten the vessel. They thus jettisoned about
two hundred tons of iron sleepers—working at this job

till midnight—and threw it over the right or starboard side of the ship, where it lay in a great mass. It was never recovered, though every effort was afterwards made to save it. It had been engulfed and disappeared in the Goodwins' capacious maw.

The men of the lifeboat, now cold, wearied, and hungry, managed to get an exceedingly frugal meal of tea and some bread and meat, and about 4 or 5 p.m. the light N.W. breeze fell away to a calm. Towards 7 p.m. the Champion lugger at anchor hoisted her light, to indicate the channel or swatchway by which the Mandalay would have to come out if ever she moved at all. The wind now came strong from the S.W. and then backed to S. and by W., and there was heard the far-off moan of breaking surf, making it plain that there was a heavy sea rolling in from the S.W. on a distant point of the Sands. The sea was evidently coming before the wind, 'the moon looked,' the men said, 'as if she was getting up contrâry,' and Roberts said, 'We'll have trouble before morning.' At 10 p.m. the wind came. The calm was 'but the grim repose of the winter whirlwind,' and it soon blew a gale from the S.W. Before this some Deal galley punts had also wisely made their way for the shore, and the lifeboat and the Champion lugger were left alone on the scene—than which nothing could now be wilder. Fortunately another tug-boat, the Cambria, had anchored about 7 p.m. in deep water outside the Goodwins, as close as was prudent to the swatchway before described; but the inevitable struggle was regarded with the greatest anxiety by all hands, notwithstanding the proffered help of the tug-boat and the lightening of the ship.

About midnight the rising tide had again covered the Goodwins, but the surface, no longer fair and calm, was now lashed into fury by the gale. The seas were breaking everywhere, and as the moon emerged from behind a flying cloud, far as the eye could see was one sheet of tumbling, raging breakers, except the narrow channel in which the brave Champion rode with her guiding light, plunging heavily even in the deep channel. But the most furious sea raged on the western jaw of the deep swatchway; there currents and cross seas met, and the breakers rose up and clashed and struck together in weightier masses and with especial fury. Now a black cloud covered the moon, and again as it swept away came the clear moonlight, but in the darkness and in the moonlight the scene was equally tremendous.

As the water deepened round the ship, sea after sea broke over her with such increasing fury that the work of jettisoning the cargo, which had been carried on under great difficulties, had to be given up, and the hatches had to be put on and battened down tight, to keep the ship from filling. The same seas that broke over the Mandalay also struck and buried the lifeboat as she rode alongside to the full scope of her cable, and as each breaker went roaring past she as regularly freed herself from the water which had been hurled into her the moment before.

At one o'clock this wild winter morning the time came for a final effort to float the ship; and the steam-tug Cambria that had been waiting outside the Sands now moved in, and, guided by the riding light of the Champion lugger, anchored for this purpose in the swatchway, was cautiously manœuvred in through the narrow channel, and feeling her way with the lead at great risk came even into the broken water in which the Mandalay was lying. This broken water was only fourteen or fifteen feet deep, and though barely enough to float the tug-boat in a sort of raging smother of froth, was not deep enough to float the Mandalay, which required three feet more and still lay firm as a rock, and, like a tide-washed rock, was swept by the seas which were flying over her.

Directed by the second coxswain, attempts were now made to get the Cambria's steel hawser on board the vessel, and in the boiling turmoil the Cambria came dangerously near the heap of jettisoned iron on the starboard side of the Mandalay. It will be plain that without the presence of the lifeboat and her crew in case of disaster, all other efforts to save the ship would have been paralysed, and indeed would never have been attempted. Without the lifeboat, no tug-boat, or any other boat, would have dared to venture into that fearful labyrinth of sand and surf.

The hawser was got on board after an hour's struggle, and made fast to the Mandalay's starboard bow; but though the Mandalay rolled and bumped she was not moved from her sandy bed. It was almost impossible for those on board to keep their feet as she struck the sand and as the seas swept her decks. The position of the tug on the starboard side of the Mandalay was so perilous that it was decided to bring her across the bows of the vessel to her port side; and this was done with great difficulty against the gale and sea continually becoming heavier. Creeping round the bows of the Mandalay the tug-boat came, and in doing so crossed the cable of the lifeboat with her hawser, and therefore the lifeboat's cable had to be slipped at once, and she had to be made fast to and ride alongside the Mandalay.

Still round came the tug, and getting into deeper water of about three or three and a half fathoms, after a most hazardous and gallant passage through the breakers round the vessel, set her engines going full speed ahead. The seas now struck and bumped the Mandalay so heavily that, in spite of all efforts to save her, she was in a most critical position, and at the same time a great disaster nearly occurred. The great steel hawser of the tug, as she strained all her powers, was now tautening and slackening, and then, as steam strove for the mastery against the storm, again tightening with enormous force till it became like a rigid iron bar. It vibrated and swung alongside the lifeboat, which could not get out of the way, and dared not leave the vessel—return to which, had the lifeboat once slipped her anchor, against wind and tide would have been impossible ; and their comrades' lives, and those of all, depended on their standing by the vessel. Though the gallant coxswain did all that man could do to combat this new danger, still with a terrific jerk the steel hawser got right under the lifeboat, hoisting her, in spite of her great weight, clean out of the water.

Aided by an awful breaker, whose tumultuous and raging advance was seen afar in the moonlight, this powerful jerk of the tightening hawser, which had got under the very keel of the lifeboat, lifted her up so high that she struck in her descent, with her ponderous iron keel or very undermost part of the lifeboat, the top rail of the Mandalay's bulwarks. The marvel is how she escaped being turned right over by the shock. The next day I saw with astonishment the crushed woodwork where this mighty blow had been struck.

The lifeboat's rudder was smashed and her great stern post sprung, and one of the crew that remained in her was also injured, but still Roberts held on to the ship. At this critical moment Hanger, seeing the lifeboat's safety was endangered, and regarding it as a question of saving not only his comrades' lives but the lives of all, most reluctantly gave orders to cut the steel hawser of the tug, which was made fast on board the vessel. This would have of course sacrificed all the trouble and risk that had been incurred ; another tug-boat had also crept up on the starboard bow to help the first, and efforts were being made to get her hawser too on board ; in fact, success and safety seemed almost within their grasp, but it was a matter of life or death, and one of the Deal men, obeying orders, seized an axe and hewed and struck with all his might at the steel hawser, which was still endangering the lifeboat.

Strand after wire strand was divided, when a great sea came and the vessel trembled from her keel to her truck, and all hands had to hold on for life. Down again came the axe, as the sea went by. But its edge was blunted and it cut slowly, as the wielder doubled his efforts in reply to the shouts, 'Cut the hawser, or the lifeboat's lost!'

A confused struggle was now going on ; some were passing the second tug-boat's hawser on board, and some were trying, under pressure of dire necessity, to cut the hawser by which the Cambria tug was straining at the vessel, and still the terrible hawser got under the lifeboat,

and still the axeman strove vainly with a blunted axe
to divide the hawser.

Another sea came racing at the vessel. It lifted her
off the Sands, and thumped her down with such fury that
Hanger said, 'The bottom is coming out of her!'

Just then, holding on to prevent himself falling, he
looked at the compass, 'Great heavens! She's moving!
She's slewing, lads!' he said; the axeman threw down
his useless axe, and again came a sea, lifting up the
vessel and her iron cargo as if she had been a feather.
Had she struck the bottom as violently as before, her
masts must have gone over with a crash into the lifeboat,
but the lift of this overwhelming sea was at the very
instant aided by the strain of the tug-boat's hawser
exerting enormous force, though divided almost in twain,
and the vessel's head was torn round to the east and,
'Hurrah! my lads! she's off!' was heard from the undaunted but wearied battlers with the storm.

The hawser of the second tug-boat had been passed
shortly before this with extreme danger both to that
tug-boat, the Iona, and to the lifeboatmen working
forwards to make it fast, on the slippery footing of the
deck. The strain of the second tug-boat was now felt
by the moving vessel, and then came the scrapes and
the crunches and the thumps as she was pulled over the
sand towards the deep swatchway. Her head sails
were set, to pay her head off still more, and at last the
victorious tug-boats pulled her safe into the swatchway,
accompanied by the lifeboat.

On the left or western jaw, it will be remembered, the
most terrific sea was running, and the tug-boat approached
this awful turmoil too closely. Fortunately, Roberts saw

the danger, and shouted from the lifeboat, 'Port your
helm! Hard a-port! or you're into the breakers!' Hanger
on board, with answering readiness, set the great spanker
of the vessel, and forced her head up to the north-east,
barely clearing the Champion and her invaluable riding
light; and at last the Mandalay was towed through the
narrow swatch, on either side of which roared the hungry
breakers, baulked of their prey by human skill and
perseverance and dauntless British pluck.

Some time before emerging from the death-trap, as
the spot where the Mandalay grounded might well be
called, and when in the very most anxious and critical
part of the struggle, the moon broke out from behind
a great dark cloud, and there was seen struggling and
labouring in the gale a ship whose sails caught the
moonlight. She shone out vividly against the black
background, but the lifeboatmen were horrified to see
that, attracted by the lights of the Champion, she was
heading straight for the terrible sea on the western jaw
of the swatch, where she apparently thought she would
find safe anchorage in company with other vessels.

The North Deal coxswain expected to see her strike,
and had decided, in his mind, to get his crew from the
Mandalay on board, and then rush through the breakers
to the doomed vessel, and having rescued her crew, to
return with the help of one of the tug-boats to the
Mandalay; but, fortunately, this catastrophe was averted
by the humane and generous action of the captain of the
tug-boat Bantam Cock, who went at full speed within
hail, and warned the unsuspecting vessel of the terrible
danger so near her.

We can almost fancy we hear the hoarse shouts from

the tug-boat of 'Breakers ahead!' 'Goodwins under your lee!' and then the rattling and the thunderous noise of the sails, and the creaking of the yards and braces, as the vessel swings round on the other tack into safety.

The Mandalay was then towed out of the swatchway by the Cambria into deep water, and round the Goodwin Sands, with the lifeboat alongside her, into the anchorage of the Downs by the half-divided hawser. Had the axe's edge been keener, or had a few more blows been struck, or a few more strands severed, or had the masts of the vessel crashed into the lifeboat, or the lifeboat been capsized by the hawser's mighty jerks, how different a tale would have been told!

But it is our happy privilege to record the successful issue of thirty-five hours' struggle against the terrors of a winter's gale on the Goodwin Sands, and of doing some small justice to the seamanlike skill and daring of the Deal coxswains and lifeboatmen, and of all engaged in the task.

It will be seen from the case recorded in this chapter that the motives which were apparent in the minds of the brave fellows who manned the lifeboat on each occasion were those of humanity and generous ardour to succour the distressed; the salvage of property was an afterthought. They started from the beach to put their intimate local knowledge of the Goodwins, their skill, their strength, nay, their lives, at the service of seamen in distress; but when they saw that their energies, and theirs alone, could save a valuable vessel and her cargo, and that they could earn such fair recompense as the law allowed, this salvage of property became a duty,

M

in the discharge of which, had any man lost his life, he would have lost it nobly. having entered upon his perilous task in the unselfish and sublimer spirit of rescuing 'some forlorn and shipwrecked brother' from death on the Goodwin Sands.

M 2

THE WRECK OF THE LEDA.

CHAPTER XI

THE LEDA

Swift on the shore, a hardy few
The Lifeboat man, with a gallant, gallant crew.

SOME years ago I remember reading a tale, the hero
of which was a youth of nineteen. The scene was laid
around the lifeboat of either Deal or Walmer. There
was supposed to be a ship in distress on the Goodwins,
and the night was dark and stormy. All the boatmen
hung back, so the story ran, from the work of rescue,
and shrank from the black fury of the gale, when the
hero appeared on the scene, and roundly rating the coxswain and crew, sprang into the lifeboat, pointed out
exactly what should be done, gave courage to all the
quailing boatmen, and seizing an oar — those heroic
youths always 'seize' or 'grasp' an oar—pulled to the
Goodwin Sands 'in the teeth of a gale.' I notice these
heroes always prefer the ' teeth of a gale,' especially when
pulling in a lifeboat; nothing would apparently induce
them to touch an oar if the wind were fair or moderate.

Having rescued the crew of the distressed vessel, *solus
fecit*—some slight assistance having also been rendered

by the lifeboatmen—the lifeboat is of course overturned, and he swims ashore. Still, by some extraordinary manœuvre on the part of the wind 'in the teeth of the gale,' bearing the beauteous heroine in his arms, with the usual result and the inevitable opposition from the cruel uncle, who is actuated of course by deadly hatred to all heroic youths of nineteen.

I only refer to this fiction to point out how absurd it is to represent the brave men who man our lifeboats of the Goodwin Sands and Downs as ever needing to be roused to action by passing and incompetent strangers, who must be as ignorant of the perils to be faced as of the work to be done. When the boatmen of Deal hang back in the storm-blast, who else dare go?

Again, the three lifeboats of this locality always *sail* to the distant Goodwin Sands. To reach those sands, four to eight miles distant, according as the wreck lies on the inner or the outer edge. in one of our heavy lifeboats, if they were only propelled by oars, would be impossible. As a matter of fact, the lifeboat services to the Goodwins are invariably effected under sail. In other places, where the wreck lies close to the land, and the lifeboats are comparatively light, services are performed with oars, but not to the Goodwin Sands, which have to be reached under sail, and from which the lifeboats have to get home by sail, often against a gale off shore, eight miles to windward—with no steam-tug to help them, but by their own unaided skill, 'heart within and God o'er-head.'

The following simple statement—far below the sublime reality—will prove, if proof be needed, that the men who live between the North and South Forelands are not

inferior to their fathers who sailed with Blake and
Nelson.

About one o'clock on Sunday, December 28, 1879, a
gun from the South Sand Head lightship, anchored
about a mile south of the Goodwins, and six miles from
Deal, gave warning that a ship was on the dreadful Sands.
It was blowing a gale from the south-west, and the ships
in the Downs were riding and straining at both anchors.
It was a gale to stop your breath, or, as the sailors say,
' to blow your teeth down your throat,' and the sea was
white with 'spin drift.' As the various congregations
were streaming out of church, umbrellas were turned
inside out, hats were blown hopelessly, wildly seawards,
and children clung to their parents for shelter from the
blinding spray along Deal beach.

Just then, in answer to the boom of the distant gun,
the bell rang to ' man the lifeboat,' and the Deal boatmen answered gallantly to the summons. A rush was
made for the lifebelts. The first and second coxwains,
Wilds and Roberts, were all ready, and prepared with
the key of the lifeboat house, as the rush of men was
made.

The first thirteen men who succeeded in getting the
belts with the two coxwains formed the crew, and down
the steep beach plunged the great lifeboat to the rescue.
There were three vessels on the Goodwins : the fate of
one is uncertain ; another was a small vessel painted
white, supposed to be a Dane, and she suddenly disappeared before my eyes, being probably lost with all
hands ; the third was a German barque, the Leda, homeward bound to Hamburg, with a crew of seventeen ' all
told.' This ill-fated vessel while flying on the wings of

the favouring sou'-westerly gale, supposed by the too partial poet to be

A ladies' breeze,
Bringing home their true loves,
Out of all the seas,

struck, while thus impelled at full speed before the wind, the inner part of the S.E. spit of the Goodwin Sands. This is a most dangerous spot, noted for the furious surf which breaks on it, and where the writer has had a hard fight for his life with the sea.

The Germans, therefore, found this 'ladies' breeze' of Charles Kingsley's splendid imagination more unfriendly to them than even 'the black north-easter,' and their first contact with the Goodwin Sands was a terrific crash while they were all at dinner, toasting absent friends and each other with the kindly German *prosit*, and harmless clinking of glasses, innocent of alcohol.

The shock against the Goodwins as the vessel slid from the crest of a snowy roller upon the Sands, threw the cabin dinner table and everything on it up to the cabin ceiling, and no words can describe the wild hurry and helpless confusion on the sea-pelted motionless vessel, as the foam and the spray beat clean over her.

Under her reefed mizzen and reefed storm foresail the lifeboat came ramping over the four miles of tempestuous sea between the mainland and the Goodwins, the sea getting bigger and breaking more at the top of each wave, or 'peeling more,' as the Deal phrase goes, the farther they went into the full fetch of the sea rolling up Channel. At last the shallower water was reached about twenty feet in depth, where the Goodwins commence.

Up to this point any ordinary good sea-boat of sufficient size and power would have made as good weather of it as the lifeboat, but when at this depth of twenty feet the great rollers from the southward began to curl and topple and break into huge foam masses, and coming from different directions to race with such enormous speed and power that the pillars of foam thrown up by the collision were seen at the distance of five miles, then no boat but a lifeboat, it should be clearly understood, could live for five minutes, and even in a lifeboat only the 'sons of the Vikings' dare to face it.

The wreck lay a long mile right into the very thick of this awful surf, into which the Deal men boldly drove the lifeboat. As her great forefoot was forced through the crest of each sea she sent showers of spray over her mast and sails, and gleamed and glistened in the evening sun as she struggled with the sea.

To the wrecked crew she was visible from afar, and her bright colours and red sails told them unmistakeably she was a lifeboat. Now buried, then borne sky-high, she appeared to them as almost an angelic being expressly sent for their deliverance, and with joy and gratitude they watched her conquering advance, and they knew that brave English hearts were guiding the noble boat to their rescue.

When within about half a mile, the lifeboatmen saw the mainmast of the vessel go over, and then down crash came the mizzenmast over the port side, carrying with them in the ruin spars and rigging in confusion, and all this wild mass still hung by the shrouds and other rigging round the quarter and stern of the doomed ship, and were ever and anon drawn against her by the sea, beating her planking with thunderous noise and tremendous force.

The Leda's head was now lying S.W., or facing the sea, as after she struck stem on, her nose remained fast, and the sea gradually beat her stern round. There was running a very strong lee-tide, i.e. a tide running in the same direction as the wind and sea, setting fiercely across the Sands and outwards across the bows of the wreck. Owing, therefore, to this strong cross tide and the great sea, every minute breaking more furiously as the water was falling with the ebb-tide, the greatest judgment was required by the coxswains to anchor in the right spot, so as not to be swung hopelessly out of reach of the vessel by the tide. All the bravery in the world would have failed to accomplish the rescue, had the requisite experience been wanting. Nothing but experience and the faculty of coming to a right decision in a moment, amidst the appalling grandeur and real danger which surrounded them, enabled the coxswains to anchor just in the right spot, having made the proper allowance for the set of the tide, the sea, and the wind.

This decision had to be made in less time than I have taken to write this sentence, and the lives of men hung thereon. All hands knew it, so 'Now! Down foresail!' and the men rushed at the sail, and some to the 'down-haul,' and got it in; the helm being put hard down, up, head to sea, came the lifeboat, and overboard went the anchor, taking with it coil after coil of the great white five-inch cable of Manilla hemp; and to this they also bent a second cable, in order to ride by a long scope. thus running out about 160 fathoms or 320 yards of cable. They dropped anchor therefore nearly a fifth of a mile ahead of the wreck and well on her starboard bow. Now bite, good anchor ! and hold fast, stout cable! for the lives of all depend on you.

If the cable parted, and the lifeboat struck the ship with full force, coming astern or broadside on, not a man would have survived to tell the tale, or if she once got astern of the wreck she could not have worked to windward - against the wind and tide—to drop down as before. No friendly steam-tug was at hand to help them to windward, in case of the failure of this their first attempt, and both the lifeboatmen and the crew of the wrecked vessel knew the stake at issue, and that this was the last chance. But the crew of the lifeboat said one to another, ' We're bound to save them,' and with all the coolness of the race, though strung to the highest pitch of excitement, veered down towards the wreck till abreast of where her mainmast had been.

Clinging to the bulwarks and forerigging in a forlorn little cluster were the Germans, waving to the lifeboat as she was gradually veered down alongside, but still at a considerable distance from the wreck and the dangerous tossing tangle of wreckage still hanging to her.

To effect communication with a wreck, the lifeboat is provided with a piece of cane as thick as a man's little finger and about a foot long, to which a lump of lead is firmly fastened. To the end of the cane a long light line is attached, and the line is kept neatly coiled in a bucket.

With this loaded cane in his right hand, a man stood on the gunwale of the lifeboat ; round his waist his comrades had passed a line, to prevent him from being washed overboard : his left hand grasped the halyards, for the masts of the lifeboat are always left standing alongside a wreck, and at the right moment with all his might he threw the cane. Hissing through the air, it carried with it right on board the wreck its own light line, which at great risk a German sailor seized. Hauling it in, he found the lifeboat had bent on to it a weightier rope, and thus communication was effected between the lifeboat and the wreck.

But though the lifeboat rode plunging alongside, she rode alongside at a distance of twenty yards from the wreck, and had to be steered and sheered, though at anchor, just as if she was in motion. At the helm, therefore, stood the two coxswains, while round the foremast and close to the fore air-box grouped the lifeboatmen. Wave after wave advanced. breaking over them in clouds, taking their breath away and drenching them.

The coxswains were watching for a smooth to sheer the lifeboat's head closer to the wreck, and the wearied sailors on the wreck were anxiously watching their efforts, when, as will happen at irregular intervals, which are beyond calculation, a great sea advanced, and was seen towering afar. ' Hold on, men, for your lives !' sang out the coxswains, and on came the hollow green sea, so far above their heads that it seemed as they gazed into its terrible transparency that the very sky had become green, and it broke into the lifeboat, hoisting her up to the vessel's foreyard, and then plunging her bodily down and down.

In this mighty hoist the port bilge-piece of the lifeboat as she descended struck the top rail of the vessel's bulwarks, and the collision stove in her fore air-box.

That she was not turned clean over by the shock, throwing out of her, and then falling on, her crew, was only by God's mercy. All attempts to help the seamen on the wreck in distress were suspended and buried in the wave. The lifeboatmen held on with both arms round the thwarts in deadly wrestle and breathless for dear life. Looking forwards as the boat emerged, the coxswains, standing aft on their raised platform, could only see boiling foam. Looking aft as the noble lifeboat emptied herself, the crew saw the two coxswains waist deep in froth, and the head of the Norman post aft was invisible and under water. We were all ' knocked silly by that sea,' said the men, and they found that two of their number had been swept aft and forced under the thwarts or seats of the lifeboat.

And now they turned to again—no one being missing —alone in that wild cauldron of waters, with undaunted courage, to the work of rescue. Two lines leading from the ship to the lifeboat were rigged up, the ends of those lines being held by one of the lifeboatmen, George Philpot, who had to tighten and slack them as the lifeboat rose, or when a sea came. Spread-eagled on this rough ladder or cat's cradle, holding on for their lives, the German crew had to come, and Philpot, who held the lines in the lifeboat—no easy task—was lashed to the lifeboat's mast, to leave his hands free and prevent his being swept overboard himself. A space of about thirty feet separated the wreck and the lifeboat, as the latter's head had to get a hard sheer off from the ship, to counterbalance the tide and sea sucking and driving her towards the wreck, and over this dangerous chasm the German sailors came.

Still the giant seas swept into the lifeboat, and again and again the lifeboat freed herself from the water, and floated buoyant, in spite of the damage done to her air-box, so great was her reserve of floating power. This her crew knew, and preserved unbounded confidence in the noble structure under their feet, especially as they heard the clicks of her valves at work and freeing her of water.

In the intervals between the raging seas, twelve of the crew had now been got into the lifeboat, when one man seeing her sheer closer than usual towards the vessel, jumped from the top rail towards the lifeboat. Instead of catching her at the propitious moment when she was balanced on the summit of a wave, he sprang when she was rapidly descending; this added ten feet to the height of his jump, and he fell groaning into the lifeboat.

Having put the rescued men on the starboard side of the lifeboat, to make room for the descent of the others, great seas again came fiercely and furiously. As the tide was falling fast, the water became shallower, and all around was heard only the hoarse roar of the storm, and there was seen only the advancing lines of billows, tossing their snowy manes as they came on with speed.

Again and again the lifeboat was submerged, and the man lashed to the mast had to ease off the lines he held till the seas had passed.

' It was as if the heavens was falling atop of us; but we had no fear then, we were all a-takin' of it as easy as if we was ashore, but it was afterwards we thought of it.'

But not so the rescued crew who were in the lifeboat; some of them wanted to get back to the ship, which was fast breaking up, but one of their number had, strange to say, been rescued before—twice before, some say—by the same lifeboat on the very same Goodwin Sands, and he encouraged his comrades and said, 'She's all right! she's done it before! Good boat! good boat!' And then the rest of the crew came down, or rather along the two lines, held fast and eased off as before, till, last man down, or rather along the lines, came the captain. 'Come along, captain! Come along. There's a booser coming!' and Roberts aft, second coxswain, strained at the helm to sheer the lifeboat off, before the sea came.

It came towering. 'Quick! Captain! Come!' Had the captain rapidly come along the lines, he would have been safe in the lifeboat, but he hesitated just for an instant, and then the sea came—a moving mountain of broken water, one of the most appalling objects in Nature—breaking over the foreyard of the wreck, sweeping everything before it on the deck, and covering lifeboat and men. Everything was blotted out by the green water, as they once again wrestled in their strong grasp of the thwarts, while the roar and smother of drowning rang in their ears. But there is One who holds the winds in His fist and the sea in the hollow of His hand, and once again by His mercy not a man was missing, and again rose the lifeboat, and gasping and half-blinded, they saw that the ropes along which the captain was coming were twisted one across the other, and that, though he had escaped the full force of the great wave, the captain of the Leda was hanging by one hand, and on the point of dropping into the wild turmoil beneath, exhausted. Another second would have been too late, when, quick as lightning, the lifeboatman,

G. Philpot, still being lashed to the mast, by a dexterous jerk, chucked one of the ropes under the leg of the clinging and exhausted man, and then, once again, they cried, 'Come along! Now's your time!' And on he came; but as the ropes again slacked as the lifeboat rose, fell into the sea, though still grasping the lines, while strong and generous hands dragged him safe into the lifeboat—the last man. All saved! And now for home!

They did not dare to haul up to their anchor, had that been possible, lest before they got sail on the lifeboat to drag her away from the wreck she should be carried back against the wreck, or under her bows, when all would have perished. So the coxswains wisely decided to set the foresail, and then when all was ready, the men all working splendidly together, 'Out axe, lads! and cut the cable!' Away to the right or starboard faintly loomed the land, five long miles distant. Between them and it raged a mile of breakers throwing up their spiky foaming crests, while their regular lines of advance were every now and then crossed by a galloping breaking billow coming mysteriously and yet furiously from another direction altogether, the result being a collision of waters and pillars and spouts of foam shot up into the air. Through this broken water they had to go—there was no other way home, and 'there are no back doors at sea.' So down came the keen axe, and the last strand of the cable was cut.

Then they hoisted just a corner of the foresail, to cast her head towards the land and away from the wreck—more they dared not hoist, lest they should capsize in such broken water, the wind still blowing very hard. As her head paid off, a big sea was seen coming high above the others. 'Haul down the foresail, quick!' was the cry; but it was too late, and the monstrous sea struck the bows and burst into the sail, filling and overpowering the lifeboat and the helm and the steersmen—for both Wilds and Roberts were straining at the yoke lines—and hurled the lifeboat like a feather right round before the wind, and she shot onwards with and amidst this sea, almost into the deadly jangle of broken masts and great yards and tops, which with all their rigging and shrouds and hamper were tossing wildly in the boiling surf astern of the wreck.

But the noble deed was not to end in disaster. Beaten and hustled as the Deal lifeboatmen were with this great sea, there was time enough for those skilled and daring men to set the foresail again, to drag her clear before they got into the wreckage. 'Sheet home the foresail, and sit steady, my lads,' said Roberts, 'and we'll soon be through!' and they made for the danger-ous broken water, which was now not more than twelve feet deep. The coxswains kept encouraging the men, 'Cheer up, my lads!' And then, 'Look out, all hands! A sea coming!' And then, 'Five minutes more and we'll be through.' And so with her goodly freight of thirty-two souls, battered but not beaten, reeling to and fro, and staggering and plunging on through the surf, each moment approaching safety and deep water—on pressed the lifeboat.

Now gleams of hope broke out as the lifeboat lived and prospered in the battle, and at last the rescued Germans saved 'from the jaws of death,' and yet hardly believing they were saved, sang out, though feeble and exhausted, 'Hurrah! Cheer, O.' And inside the

N

breakers the Kingsdown lifeboat, on their way to help, responded with an answering cheer.

Then we may be well sure that from our own silent, stubborn Deal men, many a deep-felt prayer of gratitude, unuttered it may be by the lips, was sent up from the heart to Him, the ' Eternal Father strong to save,' while the Germans now broke openly out into ' Danke Gott! Danke Gott!' and soon afterwards were landed—grateful beyond expression for their marvellous deliverance—on Deal beach[1].

With conspicuous exceptions, few notice and fewer still remember those gallant deeds done by those heroes of our coast.

Few realize that those poor men have at home an aged mother perhaps dependent on them, or children, or ' a nearer one yet and a dearer,' and that when they ' darkling face the billow' the possibility of disaster to themselves assumes a more harrowing shape, when they think of loved ones left helpless and destitute behind them.   Riches cannot remove the pang of bereavement, but alas! for ' the *comfortless* troubles of the needy, and because of the deep sighing of the poor.'   And yet the brave fellows never hang back and never falter.   There ought to be, there *is* amongst them, a trust in the living God.

They apparently think little of their own splendid deeds, and seldom speak of them, especially to strangers;

---

[1] The names of the crew who on this occasion manned the lifeboat were: Robert Wilds (coxswain 1st), R. Roberts (coxswain 2nd), Thos. Cribben, Thos. Parsons, G. Pain, Chas. Hall, Thomas Roberts, Will Baker, John Holbourn, Ed. Pain, George Philpot, R. Williams, W. Adams, H. Foster, Robt. Redsull. Of these men, poor Tom Cribben never recovered the exposure and the strain.

yet they are part, and not the least glorious part, of our 'rough island story.' The recital of them makes our hearts thrill, and revives in us the memories of our youth and our early worship of heroic daring in a righteous cause. God speed the lifeboat and her crew!

CHAPTER XII

THE D'ARTAGNAN AND THE HEDVIG SOPHIA

Loud roared the dreadful thunder,
The rain a deluge poured.

THERE was a gale from the S.W. blowing over the southern part of England, on November 11, 1877. The barometer had been low, but the 'centre of depression' was still advancing, and was probably over the Straits of Dover about the middle of the day. Perhaps more is known now than formerly of the path of the storm and the date of its arrival on these coasts, and more is also known of the pleasanter but rarer anti-cyclonic systems. Nevertheless, we are still in the dark as to the cause which originates those two different phenomena, and brings them from the east and the west. The secrets of Nature belong to Him who holds the winds in His fist and the sea in the hollow of His hand.

In the seaboard towns of the S E. coast the houses shook before the blast, and now and then the tiles crashed to the pavement, and the fierce rain squalls swept through the deserted streets, as the gale ' whistled aloft his tempest tune.' To read of this makes every fireside seem more comfortable, but somehow it also

A NIGHT SCENE ON THE GOODWINS.

brings the thought to many a heart ' God help those at sea to-night ! '

In the great roadstead of the Downs, among the pilots and the captains, there were anxious hearts that day. There were hundreds of ships at anchor, of many nations, all outward bound, and taking refuge in the comparative shelter of the Downs. Those vessels had everything made as snug as possible to meet the gale, and were mostly riding to two anchors and plunging bows under. Here and there a vessel was dragging and going into collision with some other vessel right astern of her ; or perhaps slipping both her anchors just in time to avoid the crash ; or away to the southward could be seen in the rifts of the driving rain squalls, a large ship drifting, with anchors gone and sails blown into ribbons.

Deal beach was alive with the busy crowds of boat-men either launching or beaching their luggers. The smaller boats, the galley punts, which are seven feet beam and about twenty-eight feet in length, found the wind and sea that day too much for them, especially in the afternoon. They had been struggling in the Downs all day with two or three reefs, and in the ' smokers ' with ' yardarm taken,' but in the afternoon the mercury in the barometers began to jump up and

> First rise after low
> Foretells a stronger blow.

Then the galley punts had to come ashore, and only the luggers and the ' cats ' were equal to cruising among the storm-tossed shipping, ' hovelling ' or on the look-out for a job.

Some of the vessels might need a pilot to take them

to Margate Roads or northwards, or some might require a spare yard, or men to man the pumps, or an anchor and chain, the vessels in some cases riding to their last remaining anchor—or perhaps their windlass had given way or the hawse pipe had split, and in that case their own chain cable would cut them down to the water's edge in a few hours. To meet these various needs of the vessels, the great luggers were all day being continuously beached and launched, and it was hard to say which of the two operations was most perilous to themselves or most fascinating to the spectator. Once afloat they hovered about, on the wing as it were, among the vessels, and from the beach it could be seen how crowded with men they were, and how admirably they were handled.

The skill of the Deal boatmen is generally supposed to be referred to in the lines:

> Where'er in ambush lurk the fatal sands,
> They claim the danger, proud of skilful bands;
> Fearless they combat every hostile wind,
> Wheeling in mazy tracks with course inclined.

The passage has certainly a flavour of the Goodwins, but at any rate the sea-bird does not sweep to the raging summit of a wave, or glide more easily from its seething crest down the dark deep blue slope to its windless trough, or more safely than the Deal boatmen in their luggers.

Richard Roberts had been all that day afloat in the Downs in his powerful 'cat,' the Early Morn. It was this boat, some of my readers may remember, which picked up, struggling in the water, twenty-four of the passengers of the Strathclyde, when she was run down off Dover by the Franconia, some years ago. But the gale increasing towards evening, Roberts, who had got to leeward too much, could not beat home, and he had to run away before the wind and round the North Foreland to Margate. Thence he took train, and leaving his lugger in safety, reached Deal about nine p.m., just as the flash from the Gull lightship, and then the distant boom of a gun and again another flash, proclaimed there was a ship ashore on the sands. And through the wild rain gusts he saw the flare of a vessel in distress on the Brake Sand—God have mercy on them! for well he knew the hard and rocky nature of that deadly spot.

Then rang out wildly above the storm-shriek the summons from the iron throat of the lifeboat bell, 'Man the lifeboat! Man the lifeboat!' The night was dark, the ponderous surf thundered on the shingle, and there could be seen the long advancing lines of billows breaking into white masses of foam ; and outside that there was only the blackness of sea and sky, and the tossing lights and flares and signals calling for help. 'No lanterns could be kept lit that night, sir! Blowed out they was, and we had to feel our way in the lifeboat.'

And you might hear in the bustle and din of quick preparation the boatmen's shouts, 'Ease her down, Bill! just to land her bow over the full!' 'Man that haul-off warp! she'll never get off against them seas unless you man that haul-off warp! Slack it off!' And the coxswain shouts, 'All hands aboard the lifeboat! Cut the lanyard!'

Then the trigger flies loose and the stern chain which holds the lifeboat in her position on the beach smokes through the 'ruffles,' or hole in the iron keel through which it runs, as the mighty lifeboat gains speed in her rush down the steep declivity of the beach.   As she nears the sea, faster still she slides and shoots over the well-greased skids, urged forwards by her own weight and pulled forwards by the crew, who grasp the haul-off warp moored off shore a long way, and at last, as a warrior to battle, with a final bound she meets the shock of the first great sea.   And then she vanishes into the darkness. God speed her on her glorious errand!

Close-reefed mizzen and double-reefed storm foresail was the canvas under which the lifeboat that night struggled with the storm, to reach the vessel on the Brake Sand. 'She did fly along, sir, that night, but we were too late! The flare went out when we were half-way!' Alas! alas! while the gallant crew were flying on the wings of mercy and of hope to the rescue, the vessel broke up and vanished with all hands in the deep.

The lifeboat cruised round and round in the breakers, but all in vain. The crew gazed and peered into the gloom and listened, and then they shouted all together, but they could hardly hear each other's voices, and there was no answer; all had perished, and rescue close at hand!

Suddenly there was a lift in the rain, and between them and the land they saw another flare, 'Down with the foresheet! All hands to the foresheet! Now down with the mizzen sheet!' cried the coxswain, and ten men flew to the sheets. As the lifeboat luffed she lay over to her very bearings, beating famously to windward on her second errand of mercy.

It was about midnight, and there was 'a terrible nasty sea,' and a great run under the lifeboat as she neared the land; and the coxswains made out the dim form of a large vessel burning her flare, with masts gone and the sea beating over her.

Once again the lifeboat was put about, and came up into the wind's eye, the foresail was got down and the other foresail hoisted on the other side and sheeted home, sails, sheets and blocks rattling furiously in the gale, and forwards on the other tack into the spume and sea-drift the lifeboat 'ratched.' Between them and the vessel that was burning her signal of distress, the keen eyes of the lifeboatmen discerned an object in the sea, 'not more than fifty fathoms off, as much as ever it was, it was that bitter dark!' Another wreck! 'Let us save them at any rate!' said the storm-beaten lifeboatmen, as a feeble cry was heard.

The anchor was dropped. The lifeboat was then veered down on her cable a distance of eighty fathoms, and the object in the sea was found to be a forlorn wreck. Her lee deck bulwarks were deep under water, and even her weather rail was low down to the sea.

The wreck was a French brig, the D'Artagnan, as was afterwards ascertained, and on coming close it was seen her masts were still standing, but leaning over so that her yardarms touched the water. Nothing could live long on her deck, which was half under water and swept by breakers.

In the main rigging were seen small objects, which were found to be the crew, and in answer to the shouts of the lifeboatmen they came down and crawled or clung along the sea-beaten weather rail. Half benumbed with terror and despair and lashed by ceaseless waves, they slowly came along towards the lifeboat, and the state of affairs at that moment was described by one of the lifeboatmen as, 'Yes, bitter dark it were, and rainin' heavens hard, with hurricane of wind all the time.'

The wreck lay with her head facing the mainland, from which she was about a mile distant, and which bore by compass about W.N.W. The wind and the strong tide were both in the same direction, and if the lifeboat had anchored ahead of the vessel she would have swung helplessly to leeward and been unable to reach the vessel at all. So, also, had she gone under the wreck's stern to leeward, the same tide would have swept her out of reach, to say nothing of the danger of falling masts. It was impossible to have approached her to windward, as one crash against the vessel's broadside in such a storm and sea would have perhaps cost the lives of all the crew.

They therefore steered the lifeboat's head right at the stern of the vessel, as well for the reasons given as also because the cowering figures in the rigging could be got off no other way. They could not be taken to windward nor to leeward, and therefore by the stern was the only alternative.

By managing the cable of the lifeboat and by steering her, or by setting a corner of her foresail, she would sheer up to the stern of the wreck just as the fishing machine called an otter rides abreast of the boat to which it is fast. The lifeboat's head was, therefore, pointed at the stern of the wreck, which was leaning over hard to starboard, and the lifeboatmen shouted to the crew, some in the rigging and some clutching the weather toprail, to 'come on and take our line.' But there was no response; only in the darkness they could see the men in distress slowly working their way towards the stern of the wreck.

The position of the lifeboat was very dangerous. The sea was raging right across her, and it was only the sacred flame of duty and of pity in the hearts of the daring crew of the lifeboat that kept them to their task. The swell of the sea was running landwards, and the 'send' of each great rolling wave, just on the point of breaking, would shoot the lifeboat forwards till her stem and iron forefoot would strike the transom and stern of the wreck with tremendous force. The strain and spring of the cable would then draw back the lifeboat two or three boats' lengths, and then another breaker, its white wrath visible in the pitchy darkness, would again drive the lifeboat forwards and upwards as with a giant's hand, and then crash! down and right on to the stern and even right up on the deck of the half-submerged vessel. Sometimes even half the length of the lifeboat was driven over the transom and on the sloping deck of the wreck, off which she grated back into the sea to leewards.

What pen can describe the turmoil, the danger, and the appalling grandeur of the scene, now black as Erebus, and again illumined by a blaze of lightning? And what pen can do justice to the stubborn courage that persevered in the work of rescue in spite of the difficulties which at each step sprang up?

It was now found that the crew in distress were French. In their paralysed and perished condition they could not make out what our men wanted them to do, and they did not make fast the lines thrown them. Nor had they any lines to throw, as their tackle and running gear were washed away, nor could they understand the hails of the lifeboatmen. Hence the task of saving them rested with the Deal men alone.

The Frenchmen, when they saw the lifeboat rising up and plunging literally upon their decks with terrific force, held back and hesitated, clinging to the weather rail, where their position was most perilous. A really solid sea would have swept all away, and every two or three minutes a furious breaker flew over them. Something had to be done to get them, and to get them the men in the lifeboat were determined.

Now the fore air-box of the lifeboat has a round roof like a tortoise's back, and there is a very imperfect hand-hold on it.

Indeed, to venture out on this air-box in ordinary weather is by no means prudent, but on this night, when it was literally raked by weighty seas sufficient in strength to tear a limpet from its grip, the peril of doing so was extreme, but still, out on that fore air-box, determined to do or die, crept Richard Roberts, at that time the second coxswain of the lifeboat, leading the forlorn hope of rescue, and not counting his life dear to him. Up as the lifeboat rose, and down with her into the depths, still Roberts held on with the tenacity of a sailor's grasp.

As the lifeboat surged forwards on the next sea, held behind by his comrades' strong arms, out on the very stem he groped his way, and then he shouted, and behind him all hands shouted, 'Come, Johnny! Now's your time!' There's a widespread belief among our sailor friends that the expression 'Johnny' is a passport to a Frenchman's heart. At any rate, seeing Roberts on the very stem and hearing the shouts, the nearly exhausted Frenchmen came picking their dangerous way and clinging to the weather rail one by one till they grasped or rather madly clutched at Roberts' outstretched arms. 'Hold on, mates!' he cried, 'there's a sea coming! Don't let them drag me overboard!' And then the Frenchmen grasped Roberts' arms and chest so fiercely that his clothes were torn and he himself marked black and blue. Then rang out as each poor sailor was grasped by Roberts, 'Hurrah! I've got him! Pass him along, lads!' — and the poor fellows were rescued and welcomed by English hearts and English hands. 'We never knowed if there was any more, but at any rate we saved five,' said the lifeboatmen.

Having rescued this crew, all eyes were now turned to the vessel that had for some hours been burning her signals of distress.

It was by this time four o'clock on this winter morning, and the crew of the lifeboat were, to use their own words, 'nearly done.' They also noticed that the lifeboat was much lower than usual in the water, but neither danger, nor hardships, nor fatigue can daunt the spirits of the brave, and their courage rose above the terror of the storm, and they forgot the crippled condition of the lifeboat—both of her bows being completely stove in by the force of her blows against the deck and the transom of the French brig—and they responded gallantly to the coxswain's orders of 'Up anchor and set the foresail!' and they made for the flaré of the fresh wreck for which they had been originally heading.

The signals of distress were from a Swedish barque, the Hedvig Sophia. She had parted her anchors in the Downs, and had come ashore in three fathoms of water, which was now angry surf; her masts were gone, but as the rigging was not cut adrift, they were still lying to leeward in wild confusion. She had heeled over to starboard, and her weather rail being well out of the water, afforded some shelter to the crew; but her sloping decks were washed and beaten by the waves that broke over her and it was all but impossible to walk on them.

The lifeboat's anchor was dropped, and again they veered down, but this time it was possible to get to windward, and by reason of the wreckage it was impossible to get to leeward. There was an English pilot on board, who helped to carry out the directions given from the lifeboat, and lines were quickly passed from the wreck.

It was seen the captain's wife was on board, for the grey morning was breaking, and as the lifeboat rose on the crest of a wave, after the crew and just before the captain, who came last, the poor lady was passed into the lifeboat.

She only came with great reluctance and after much persuasion, as the deck of the lifeboat was covered with three inches of water and she seemed to be sinking. When the Swedish captain came on board, while the spray was flying sky-high over them, could he truly be said to be taken 'on board'?

'Here's a pretty thing to come in—full of water!' said the captain.

'Well,' replied Roberts, 'we've been in it all night, and you won't have to wait long.'

The lifeboatmen then got up anchor, and with twelve Swedes, five Frenchmen, and their own crew of fifteen made for home. Deep plunged the lifeboat, and wearily she rose at each sea, but still she struggled towards Deal, as the wounded stag comes home to die. Her fore and after air-boxes were full of water, for a man could creep into the rent in her bows, and she had lost much of her buoyancy. Still she had a splendid reserve in hand, from the air-boxes ranged along and under her deck, and thus fighting her way with her freight of thirty-two souls, at last she grounded on the sands off Deal, and the lifeboatmen leaped out and carried the rescued foreigners literally into England from the sea, where they were received as formerly another ship-wrecked stranger in another island 'with no little kindness.'

The next day the storm was over; sea and sky were bathed in sunshine, and the swift-winged breezes just rippled the surface of the deep into the countless dimples of blue and gold.

$$\text{Ποντίων τε κυμάτων}$$
$$\text{'Ανήριθμον γέλασμα}$$

was the exact description, more easily felt than trans-lated; but close to the North Bar buoy, in deep water, and just outside the Brake Sand, there projected from out of the smiling sea the grim stern spectacle of the masts of a barque whose hull lay deep down on its sandy bed. She it was which had been burning flares for help the night before in vain, and she had been beaten off the Brake Sand and sank before the lifeboat came. She was a West India barque, with a Gravesend pilot on board, and his pilot flag was found hoisted in

the unusual position of the mizzen topmast head, a fact
which was interpreted by the Deal boatmen as a message
—a last message to his friends, and as much as to say,
' It's me that's gone.'

But the brave men in the lifeboat did their best, and
by their extraordinary exertions, although they did not
reach this poor lost barque in time, yet by God's
blessing on their skill and daring they did save, Swedes
and Frenchmen, seventeen souls that night from a
watery grave.

COMING HOME. 'ALL SAVED.'

CHAPTER XIII

THE RAMSGATE LIFEBOAT

Not once or twice in our rough island story
The path of duty was the way to glory.

A BOOK bearing the title of *Heroes of the Goodwin Sands*, would hardly be complete without a chapter devoted to the celebrated Ramsgate lifeboat and her brave coxswain and crew. To them, by virtue of Mr. Gilmore's well-known book, the title of *Storm Warriors* almost of right belongs, but I am well aware they will not deny their daring and generous rivals of Deal a share in that stirring appellation, and I know that their friends, the Deal boatmen, on their part gladly admit that the Ramsgate lifeboatmen are also among the 'Heroes of the Goodwin Sands.'

The first lifeboat placed in Ramsgate was called the Northumberland. The next was called the Bradford, in memory of the interesting fact that the money required to build and equip her, about £600, was subscribed in an hour on the Bradford Exchange, and within the hour the news was flashed to London. Since then the rescues

effected by the Ramsgate lifeboat have become house-
hold words wherever the English tongue is spoken.

Nor less celebrated than the lifeboat is her mighty
and invaluable ally the steam-tug Aid, so often captained
in the storm-blast by Alfred Page, her brave and experienced master.   This powerful tug-boat has steam up
night and day, ready to rush the lifeboat out into the
teeth of any gale, when it would be otherwise impossible
for the lifeboat to get out of the harbour.   The names
of Coxswain Jarman, and more recently of Coxswain
Charles Fish, the hero of the Indian Chief rescue, will long
thrill the hearts of Englishmen and Englishwomen who
read that wondrous story of the sea.   It may be fairly
said that no storms that blow in these latitudes can keep
the Ramsgate tug and lifeboat back, when summoned to
the rescue.

I had the privilege of standing on Ramsgate pier-
head on November 11, 1891, when amidst the cheers of
the crowd, who indeed could hardly keep their feet, the tug
and lifeboat slowly struggled out against the great gale
which blew that day.   The lifeboat is towed a long way
astern of the tug-boat, to the full scope of a sixty fathom,
five inch, white Manilla hawser, and on the day I speak
of, as the lifeboat felt the giant strain of the tug-boat and
was driven into the seas outside the harbour, every wave
broke into wild spray mast high over the lifeboat and
into the faces of her crew.

The crew are obtained from a body of 150 enrolled
volunteers.   The first ten of these who get into the lifeboat when the rocket signal goes up from the pier-head
form on that occasion the crew of the lifeboat.   In ad-
dition to these the two coxswains, by virtue of their

office, raise the total number to twelve. The celebrated coxswain, Charles Fish, was also harbour boatman at Ramsgate, and slept in a watch-house at the end of the pier in a hammock. He was always first aroused by the watch to learn that rockets were going up from some distant lightship signifying 'a ship on the Goodwins.' With him rested the decision to send up the answering rocket from the pier-head, upon seeing which the police and coastguard called the lifeboat crew. Then would come the rush for a place.

The coxswain had to decide what signals were to be regarded as false alarms, and there are many such ; sometimes, it is said in Ramsgate, the flash of the Calais lighthouse is taken for a ship burning flares and in distress on the Goodwins, and draws the signal guns from the lightships. Sometimes a hayrick on fire is mistaken for a vessel's appealing signal ; sometimes the signals, of enormous and unnecessary size, which the French trawlers burn to each other at night around the Goodwins, set both the lightships and lifeboats all astray; and the coxswains of the lifeboats, both at Ramsgate and Deal, have to be on their guard against these delusive agencies. As the coxswains in both of these places are men of exceptional shrewdness and ability, mistakes are few and far between. The coxswain of a lifeboat ought to have the eye of a hawk and the heart of a lion, and, I will add, the tenderness and pity of a woman.

Never was the possession of these qualities more finely exhibited than by coxswain Charles Fish and the crew of the Ramsgate lifeboat in the rescue of the survivors of the Indian Chief from the Long Sand on January 5 and 6, 1881. The following account has been taken by permission from the *Lifeboat Journal* for February, 1881, including the extracts from the *Daily Telegraph* and the admirable engraving.

The accompanying graphic accounts of the wreck of the Indian Chief, and of the noble rescue of a portion of her crew by the Bradford self-righting lifeboat, stationed at Ramsgate, appeared in the *Daily Telegraph* on January 11 and 18, as related by the mate of the vessel and the coxswain of the lifeboat. The lifeboats of the National Lifeboat Institution stationed at Aldborough (Suffolk), Clacton and Harwich (Essex), also proceeded to the scene of danger, but unfortunately were unable to reach the wreck. Happily the Bradford lifeboat persevered, amidst difficulties, hardships, and dangers hardly ever surpassed in the lifeboat service ; but her reward was indeed great in saving eleven of our fellow-creatures, who must have succumbed, as their mates had a few hours previously, to their terrible exposure in bitterly cold weather for nearly thirty hours.

Indeed, Captain Braine, the zealous Ramsgate harbour-master, states in an official letter of January 8, in reference to this noble service, that—

' Of all the meritorious services performed by the Ramsgate tug and lifeboat, I consider this one of the best. The decision the coxswain and crew arrived at to remain till daylight, which was in effect to continue for fourteen hours cruising about with the sea continually breaking over them in a heavy gale and tremendous sea, proves, I consider, their gallantry and determination to do their duty. The coxswain and crew of the lifeboat speak in the highest terms of her good qualities ; they state that when sailing across the Long Sand, after leaving the wreck, the seas were tremendous, and the boat behaved most admirably. Some of the shipwrecked crew have since stated that they were fearful, on seeing the frightful-looking seas they were passing through, that they were in more danger in the lifeboat than when lashed to the mast of their sunken ship, as they thought it impossible for any boat to live through such a sea.'

The following are the newspaper accounts of a lifeboat service that will always be memorable in the annals of the services of the lifeboats of the National Lifeboat Institution ; and many and many such services reflect honour alike on the humanity of the age in which we live, and on the organisation and liberality which have prompted and called them into existence.

'On the afternoon of Thursday, January 6, I made one of a great crowd assembled on the Ramsgate east pier to witness the arrival of the survivors of the crew of a large ship which had gone ashore on the Long Sand early on the preceding Wednesday morning. A heavy gale had been blowing for two days from the north and east ; it had moderated somewhat at noon, but still stormed fiercely over the surging waters, though a brilliant blue sky arched overhead and a sun shone that made the sea a dazzling surface of broken silver all away in the south and west. Plunging bows under as she came along, the steamer towed the lifeboat through a haze of spray ; but amid this veil of foam, the flags of the two vessels denoting that shipwrecked men were in the boat streamed like well-understood words from the mastheads. The people crowded thickly about the landing-steps when the lifeboat entered the harbour.

Whispers flew from mouth to mouth. Some said the rescued men were Frenchmen, others that they were Danes, but all were agreed that there was a dead body among them. One by one the survivors came along the pier, the most dismal procession it was ever my lot to behold—eleven live but scarcely living men, most of them clad in oilskins, and walking with bowed backs, drooping heads and nerveless arms. There was blood on the faces of some, circled with a white encrustation of salt, and this same salt filled the hollows of their eyes and streaked their hair with lines which looked like snow. The first man, who was the chief mate, walked leaning heavily on the arm of the kindly-hearted harbour-master, Captain Braine. The second man, whose collar-bone was broken, moved as one might suppose a gal-vanised corpse would. A third man's wan face wore a forced smile, which only seemed to light up the piteous, underlying expression of the features. They were all saturated with brine ; they were soaked with sea-water to the very marrow of the bones. Shivering, and with a stupefied rolling of the eyes, their teeth clenched, their chilled fingers pressed into the palms of their hands, they passed out of sight. As the last man came I held my breath ; he was alive when taken from the wreck, but had died in the boat. Four men bore him on their shoulders, and a flag flung over the face mercifully con-cealed what was most shocking of the dreadful sight ; but they had removed his boots and socks to chafe his feet before he died, and had slipped a pair of mittens over the toes, which left the ankles naked. This was the body of Howard Primrose Fraser, the second mate of the lost ship, and her drowned captain's brother. I had often met men newly-rescued from shipwreck, but never remember having beheld more mental anguish and physical suffering than was expressed in the countenances and movements of these eleven sailors. Their story as told to me is a striking and memorable illustration of endurance and hardship on the one hand, and of the finest heroical humanity on the other, in every sense worthy to be known to the British public. I got the whole narrative direct from the chief mate, Mr. William Meldrum Lloyd, and it shall be related here as nearly as possible in his own words.

No. 1.—*The Mate's Account.*

'Our ship was the Indian Chief, of 1238 tons register; our skipper's name was Fraser, and we were bound with a general cargo to Yokohama. There were twenty-nine souls on board, counting the North-country pilot. We were four days out from Middlesbrough, but it had been thick weather ever since the afternoon of the Sunday on which we sailed. All had gone well with us, however, so far, and on Wednesday morning, at half-past two, we made the Knock Light. You must know, sir, that hereabouts the water is just a network of shoals; for to the southward lies the Knock, and close over against it stretches the Long Sand, and beyond, down to the westward, is the Sunk Sand. Shortly after the Knock Light had hove in sight, the wind shifted to the eastward and brought a squall of rain. We were under all plain sail at the time, with the exception of

the royals, which were furled, and the main sail that
hung in the buntlines. The Long Sand was to leeward,
and finding that we were drifting that way the order was
given to put the ship about. It was very dark, the wind
breezing up sharper and sharper, and cold as death.
The helm was put down, but the main braces fouled,
and before they could be cleared the vessel had missed
stays and was in irons. We then went to work to wear
the ship, but there was much confusion, the vessel heeling
over, and all of us knew that the Sands were close
aboard. The ship paid off, but at a critical moment the
spanker-boom sheet fouled the wheel; still, we managed
to get the vessel round, but scarcely were the braces
belayed and the ship on the starboard tack, when she
struck the ground broadside on. She was a soft-wood
built ship, and she trembled, sir, as though she would
go to pieces at once like a pack of cards. Sheets and
halliards were let go, but no man durst venture aloft.
Every moment threatened to bring the spars crushing
about us, and the thundering and beating of the canvas
made the masts buckle and jump like fishing-rods. We
then kindled a great flare and sent up rockets, and our
signals were answered by the Sunk Lightship and the
Knock. We could see one another's faces in the light
of the big blaze, and sung out cheerily to keep our
hearts up; and, indeed, sir, although we all knew that
our ship was hard and fast and likely to leave her bones
on that sand, we none of us reckoned upon dying. The
sky had cleared, the easterly wind made the stars sharp
and bright, and it was comforting to watch the lightships' rockets rushing up and bursting into smoke and
sparks over our heads, for they made us see that our

position was known, and they were as good as an assurance that help would come along soon and that we need not lose heart. But all this while the wind was gradually sweeping up into a gale—and oh, the cold, good Lord! the bitter cold of that wind!

'It seemed as long as a month before the morning broke, and just before the grey grew broad in the sky, one of the men yelled out something, and then came sprawling and splashing aft to tell us that he had caught sight of the sail of a lifeboat[1] dodging among the heavy seas. We rushed to the side to look, half-blinded by the flying spray and the wind, and clutching at whatever offered to our hands, and when at last we caught sight of the lifeboat we cheered, and the leaping of my heart made me feel sick and deathlike. As the dawn brightened we could see more plainly, and it was frightful to notice how the men looked at her, meeting the stinging spray borne upon the wind without a wink of the eye, that they might not lose sight of the boat for an instant; the salt whitening their faces all the while like a layer of flour as they watched. She was a good distance away, and she stood on and off, on and off, never coming closer, and evidently shirking the huge seas which were now boiling around us. At last she hauled her sheet

[1] This clearly is an error, for no lifeboat could possibly have been near the wreck at this early hour. The ship struck at half-past two o'clock on the morning of January 5, and at daybreak the rescue mentioned was attempted, clearly, by a smack, for no lifeboat heard of the wreck until eleven o'clock of the same day. Probably it was that smack which afterwards conveyed the news of the wreck to Harwich at 11 a.m. Another fishing smack proceeded at once to Ramsgate, and arrived there at noon, having received the information of the wreck from the Kentish Knock lightship.

aft, put her helm over, and went away. One of our crew groaned, but no other man uttered a sound, and we returned to the shelter of the deckhouses.

'Though the gale was not at its height when the sun rose, it was not far from it. We plucked up spirits again when the sun shot out of the raging sea, but as we lay broadside on to the waves, the sheets of flying water soon made the sloping decks a dangerous place for a man to stand on, and the crew and officers kept the shelter of the deck-cabins, though the captain and his brother and I were constantly going out to see if any help was coming. But now the flood was making, and this was a fresh and fearful danger, as we all knew, for at sunrise the water had been too low to knock the ship out of her sandy bed, but as the tide rose it lifted the vessel, bumping and straining her frightfully. The pilot advised the skipper to let go the starboard anchor, hoping that the set of the tide would slue the ship's stern round, and make her lie head on to the seas ; so the anchor was dropped, but it did not alter the position of the ship. To know, sir, what the cracking and strain-ing of that vessel was like, as bit by bit she slowly went to pieces, you must have been aboard of her. When she broke her back a sort of panic seized many of us, and the captain roared out to the men to get the boats over, and see if any use could be made of them. Three boats were launched, but the second boat, with two hands in her, went adrift, and was instantly engulphed, and the poor fellows in her vanished just as you might blow out a light. The other boats filled as soon as they touched the water. There was no help for us in that way, and again we withdrew to the cabins.

' A little before five o'clock in the afternoon a huge sea
swept over the vessel, clearing the decks fore and aft,
and leaving little but the uprights of the deck-houses
standing. It was a dreadful sea, but we knew worse
was behind it, and that we must climb the rigging if we
wanted to prolong our lives. The hold was already full
of water, and portions of the deck had been blown out,
so that everywhere great yawning gulfs met the eye,
with the black water washing almost flush. Some of the
men made for the fore-rigging, but the captain shouted to
all hands to take to the mizzenmast, as that one, in his
opinion, was the securest. A number of the men who
were scrambling forward returned on hearing the captain
sing out, but the rest held on and gained the foretop.
Seventeen of us got over the mizzentop, and with our
knives fell to hacking away at such running gear as
we could come at to serve as lashings. None of us
touched the mainmast, for we all knew, now the ship
had broken her back, that that spar was doomed, and
the reason why the captain had called to the men to
come aft was because he was afraid that when the
mainmast went it would drag the foremast, that rocked
in its step with every move, with it. I was next the
captain in the mizzentop, and near him was his brother,
a stout-built, handsome young fellow, twenty-two years
old, as fine a specimen of the English sailor as ever
I was shipmate with. He was calling about him cheer-
fully, bidding us not be down-hearted, and telling us
to look sharply around for the lifeboats. He helped
several of the benumbed men to lash themselves, saying
encouraging things to them as he made them fast. As
the sun sank the wind grew more freezing, and I saw the

strength of some of the men lashed over me leaving them fast. The captain shook hands with me, and, on the chance of my being saved, gave me some messages to take home, too sacred to be written down, sir. He likewise handed me his watch and chain, and I put them in my pocket. The canvas streamed in ribbons from the yards, and the noise was like a continuous roll of thunder overhead. It was dreadful to look down and watch the decks ripping up, and notice how every sea that rolled over the wreck left less of her than it found.

'The moon went quickly away—it was a young moon with little power—but the white water and the starlight kept the night from being black, and the frame of the vessel stood out like a sketch done in ink every time the dark seas ran clear of her and left her visible upon the foam. There was no talking, no calling to one another, the men hung in the topmast rigging like corpses, and I noticed the second mate to windward of his brother in the top, sheltering him, as best he could, poor fellow, with his body from the wind that went through our skins like showers of arrows. On a sudden I took it into my head to fancy that the mizzenmast wasn't so secure as the foremast. It came into my mind like a fright, and I called to the captain that I meant to make for the foretop. I don't know whether he heard me or whether he made any answer. Maybe it was a sort of craze of mine for the moment, but I was wild with eagerness to leave that mast as soon as ever I began to fear for it. I cast my lashings adrift and gave a look at the deck, and saw that I must not go that way if I did not want to be drowned. So I swung myself into the

crosstrees, and swung myself on to the stay, so reaching
the maintop, and then I scrambled on to the main topmast
crosstrees, and went hand over hand down the topmast
stay into the foretop. Had I reflected before I left the
mizzentop, I should not have believed that I had the
strength to work my way for'rards like that; my hands
felt as if they were skinned and my finger-joints appeared to have no use in them. There were nine or ten
men in the foretop, all lashed and huddled together.
The mast rocked sharply, and the throbbing of it to the
blowing of the great tatters of canvas was a horrible
sensation. From time to time they sent up rockets
from the Sunk lightship—once every hour, I think—
but we had long since ceased to notice those signals.
There was not a man but thought his time was come,
and, though death seemed terrible when I looked down
upon the boiling waters below, yet the anguish of the
cold almost killed the craving for life.

'It was now about three o'clock on Thursday morning;
the air was full of the strange, dim light of the foam and
the stars, and I could very plainly see the black swarm
of men in the top and rigging of the mizzenmast. I was
looking that way, when a great sea fell upon the hull of
the ship with a fearful crash; a moment after, the mainmast went. It fell quickly, and as it fell it bore down
the mizzenmast. There was a horrible noise of splinter-
ing wood and some piercing cries, and then another
great sea swept over the after-deck, and we who were in
the foretop looked and saw the stumps of the two masts
sticking up from the bottom of the hold, the mizzenmast
slanting over the bulwarks into the water, and the men
lashed to it drowning. There never was a more shock-

P

ing sight, and the wonder is that some of us who saw it did not go raving mad. The foremast still stood, complete to the royal mast and all the yards across, but every instant I expected to find myself hurling through the air. By this time the ship was completely gutted, the upper part of her a mere frame of ribs, and the gale still blew furiously; indeed, I gave up hope when the mizzenmast fell and I saw my shipmates drowning on it.

'It was half an hour after this that a man, who was jammed close against me, pointed out into the darkness and cried in a wild hoarse voice, "Isn't that a steamer's light?" I looked, but what with grief and suffering and cold, I was nearly blinded, and could see nothing. But presently another man called out that he could see a light, and this was echoed by yet another; so I told them to keep their eyes upon it and watch if it moved. They said by and by that it was stationary; and though we could not guess that it meant anything good for us, yet this light heaving in sight and our talking of it gave us some comfort. When the dawn broke we saw the smoke of a steamer, and agreed that it was her light we had seen; but I made nothing of that smoke, and was looking heartbrokenly at the mizzenmast and the cluster of drowned men washing about it, when a loud cry made me turn my head, and then I saw a lifeboat under a reefed foresail heading direct for us. It was a sight, sir, to make one crazy with joy, and it put the strength of ten men into every one of us. A man named Gillmore —I think it was Gillmore—stood up and waved a long strip of canvas. But I believe they had seen there were living men aboard us before that signal was made.

'The boat had to cross the broken water to fetch us, and in my agony of mind I cried out, "She'll never face it! She'll leave us when she sees that water!" for the sea was frightful all to windward of the Sand and over it, a tremendous play of broken waters, raging one with another, and making the whole surface resemble a boiling cauldron. Yet they never swerved a hair's-breadth. Oh, sir, she was a noble boat! We could see her crew —twelve of them—sitting at the thwarts, all looking our way, motionless as carved figures, and there was not a stir among them as, in an instant, the boat leapt from the crest of a towering sea right into the monstrous broken tumble.

'The peril of these men, who were risking their lives for ours, made us forget our own situation. Over and over again the boat was buried, but as regularly did she emerge with her crew fixedly looking our way, and their oilskins and the light-coloured side of the boat sparkling in the sunshine, while the coxswain, leaning forward from the helm, watched our ship with a face of iron.

'By this time we knew that this boat was here to save us, and that she *would* save us, and, with wildly beating hearts, we unlashed ourselves, and dropped over the top into the rigging. We were all sailors, you see, sir, and knew what the lifeboatmen wanted, and what was to be done. Swift as thought we had bent a number of ropes' ends together, and securing a piece of wood to this line, threw it overboard, and let it drift to the boat. It was seized, a hawser made fast, and we dragged the great rope on board. By means of this hawser the lifeboat-men hauled their craft under our quarter, clear of the

P 2

raffle. But there was no such rush made for her as might be thought. No! I owe it to my shipmates to say this. Two of them shinned out upon the mizzenmast to the body of the second mate, that was lashed eight or nine feet away over the side, and got him into the boat before they entered it themselves. I heard the coxswain of the boat—Charles Fish by name, the fittest man in the world for that berth and this work—cry out, " Take that poor fellow in there!" and he pointed to the body of the captain, who was lashed in the top with his arms over the mast, and his head erect and his eyes wide open. But one of our crew called out, "He's been dead four hours, sir," and then the rest of us scrambled into the boat, looking away from the dreadful group of drowned men that lay in a cluster round the prostrate mast.

' The second mate was still alive, but a maniac ; it was heartbreaking to hear his broken, feeble cries for his brother, but he lay quiet after a bit, and died in half an hour, though we chafed his feet and poured rum into his mouth, and did what men in our miserable plight could for a fellow-sufferer. Nor were we out of danger yet, for the broken water was enough to turn a man's hair grey to look at. It was a fearful sea for us men to find ourselves in the midst of, after having looked at it from a great height, and I felt at the beginning almost as though I should have been safer on the wreck than in that boat. Never could I have believed that so small a vessel could meet such a sea and live. Yet she rose like a duck to the great roaring waves which followed her, draining every drop of water from her bottom as she was hove up, and falling with terrible suddenness into a hollow, only to bound like a living thing to the summit of the next gigantic crest.

'When I looked at the lifeboat's crew and thought of our situation a short while since, and our safety now, and how to rescue us these great-hearted men had imperilled their own lives, I was unmanned; I could not thank them, I could not trust myself to speak. They told us they had left Ramsgate Harbour early on the preceding afternoon, and had fetched the Knock at dusk, and not seeing our wreck had lain to in that raging sea, suffering almost as severely as ourselves, all through the piercing tempestuous night. What do you think of such a service, sir? How can such devoted heroism be written of, so that every man who can read shall know how great and beautiful it is? Our own sufferings came to us as a part of our calling as seamen. But theirs was bravely courted and endured for the sake of their fellow-creatures. Believe me, sir, it was a splendid piece of service; nothing grander in its way was ever done before, even by Englishmen. I am a plain seaman, and can say no more about it all than this. But when I think of what must have come to us eleven men before another hour had passed, if the lifeboat crew had not run down to us, I feel like a little child, sir, and my heart grows too full for my eyes.'

Two days had elapsed (continues the writer in the *Daily Telegraph*) since the rescue of the survivors of the crew of the Indian Chief, and I was gazing with much interest at the victorious lifeboat as she lay motionless upon the water of the harbour. It was a very calm day, the sea stretching from the pier-sides as smooth as a piece of green silk, and growing vague in the wintry haze of the horizon, while the white cliffs were brilliant with the silver sunshine. It filled the mind with strange and moving thoughts to look at that sleeping lifeboat, with her image as sharp as a coloured photograph shining in the clear water under her, and then reflect upon the furious conflict she had been concerned in only two nights before, the freight of half-drowned men that had loaded her, the dead body on her thwart, the bitter cold of the howling gale, the deadly peril that had attended every heave of the huge black seas. Within a few hundred yards of her lay the tug, the sturdy steamer that had towed her to the Long Sand, that had held her astern all night, and brought her back safe on the following afternoon. The tug had suffered much from the frightful tossing she had received, and her injuries had not yet been dealt with; she had lost her sponsons, her starboard side-house was gone, the port side of her bridge had been started and the iron railing warped, her decks still seemed dank from the remorseless washing, her funnel was brown with rust, and the tough craft looked a hundred years old. Remembering what these vessels had gone through, how they had but two days since topped a long series of merciful and dangerous errands by as brilliant an act of heroism and humanity as any on record, it was difficult to behold them without a quickened pulse. I recalled the coming ashore of their crews, the lifeboatmen with their great cork-jackets around them, the steamer's men in streaming oilskins, the faces of many of them livid with the cold, their eyes dim with the bitter vigil they had kept and the furious blowing of the spray; and I remembered the bright smile that here and there lighted up the weary faces, as first one and then another caught sight of a wife or a sister in the crowd waiting to greet and accompany the brave hearts to the warmth of their humble homes. I felt that while these crews' sufferings and the courage and resolution they had shown remained unwritten, only half of the very stirring and manful story had been recorded. The narrative, as related to me by the coxswain of the lifeboat, is a necessary pendant to the tale told by the mate of the wrecked ship; and as he and his colleagues, both of the lifeboat and the steam-tug, want no better introduction than their own deeds to the sympathy and attention of the public, let Charles Edward Fish begin his yarn without further preface.

No. 2.—*The Coxswain's Account.*

'News had been brought to Ramsgate, as you know, sir, that a large ship was ashore on the Long Sand, and Captain Braine, the harbour-master, immediately ordered the tug and lifeboat to proceed to her assistance. It was blowing a heavy gale of wind, though it came much harder some hours afterwards; and the moment we were clear of the piers we felt the sea. Our boat is considered a very fine one. I know there is no better on the coasts, and there are only two in Great Britain bigger. She was presented to the Lifeboat Institution by Bradford, and is called after that town. But it is ridiculous to talk of bigness when it means only forty-two feet long, and when a sea is raging round you heavy enough to swamp a line-of-battle ship. I had my eye on the tug—named the Vulcan, sir—when she met the first of the seas, and she was thrown up like a ball, and you could see her starboard paddle revolving in the air high enough out for a coach to pass under; and when she struck the hollow she dished a sea over her bows that left only the stern of her showing. We were towing head to wind, and the water was flying over the boat in clouds. Every man of us was soaked to the skin, in spite of our overalls, by the time we had brought the Ramsgate Sands abeam; but there were a good many miles to be gone over before we should fetch the Knock lightship, and so you see, sir, it was much too early for us to take notice that things were not over and above comfortable.

'We got out the sail-cover—a piece of tarpaulin—to make a shelter of, and rigged it up against the mast, seizing it to the burtons; but it hadn't been up two minutes when a heavy sea hit and washed it right aft in rags; so there was nothing to do but to hold on to the thwarts and shake ourselves when the water came over. I never remember a colder wind. I don't say this because I happened to be out in it. Old Tom Cooper, one of the best boatmen in all England, sir, who made one of our crew, agreed with me that it was more like a flaying machine than a natural gale of wind. The feel of it in the face was like being gnawed by a dog. I only wonder it didn't freeze the tears it fetched out of our eyes. We were heading N.E., and the wind was blowing from N.E. The North Foreland had been a bit of shelter, like; but when we had gone clear of that, and the ocean lay ahead of us, the seas were furious— they seemed miles long, sir, like an Atlantic sea, and it was enough to make a man hold his breath to watch how the tug wallowed and tumbled into them. I sung out to Dick Goldsmith, " Dick," I says, " she's slowed, do you see, she'll never be able to meet it," for she had slackened her engines down into a mere crawl, and I really did think they meant to give up. I could see Alf Page—the master of her, sir—on the bridge, coming and going like the moon when the clouds sweep over it, as the seas smothered him up one moment, and left him shining in the sun the next. But there was to be no giving up with the tug's crew any more than with the lifeboat's; she held on, and we followed.

' Somewhere abreast of the Elbow buoy a smack that was running ported her helm to speak us. Her skipper had just time to yell out, " A vessel on the Long Sand!" and we to wave our hands, when she was astern and out of sight in a haze of spray. Presently a collier named the Fanny, with her foretopgallant-yard gone, passed us. She was cracking on to bring the news of the wreck to Ramsgate, and was making a heavy sputter under her topsails and foresail. They raised a cheer, for they knew our errand, and then, like the smack, in a minute she was astern and gone. By this time the cold and the wet and the fearful plunging were beginning to tell, and one of the men called for a nip of rum. The quantity we generally take is half a gallon, and it is always my rule to be sparing with that drink for the sake of the ship-wrecked men we may have to bring home, and who are pretty sure to be in greater need of the stuff than us.

I never drink myself, sir, and that's one reason, I think,
why I manage to meet the cold and wet middling well,
and rather better than some men who look stronger than
me.   However, I told Charlie Verrion to measure the
rum out and serve it round, and it would have made you
laugh, I do believe, sir, to have seen the care the men
took of the big bottle—Charlie cocking his finger into
the cork-hole, and Davy Berry clapping his hand over
the pewter measure, whenever a sea came, to prevent the
salt water from spoiling the liquor.   Bad as our plight
was, the tug's crew were no better off; their wheel is
forrard, and so you may suppose the fellow that steered
had his share of the seas; the others stood by to relieve
him; and for the matter of water, she was just like a
rock, the waves striking her bows and flying pretty nigh
as high as the top of her funnel, and blowing the whole
length of her aft with a fall like the tumble of half-a-
dozen cartloads of bricks.   I like to speak of what they
went through, for the way they were knocked about was
something fearful, to be sure.

'By half-past four o'clock in the afternoon it was
drawing on dusk, and about that hour we sighted the
revolving light of the Kentish Knock lightship, and a
little after five we were pretty close to her.   She is a
big red-hulled boat, with the words 'Kentish Knock'
written in long white letters on her sides, and, dark as it
was, we could see her flung up, and rushing down fit to
roll her over and over; and the way she pitched and
went out of sight, and then ran up on the black heights of
water, gave me a better notion of the fearfulness of that
sea than I had got by watching the tug or noticing our
own lively dancing.   The tug hailed her first, and two

men looking over her side answered ; but what they said didn't reach us in the lifeboat. Then the steamer towed us abreast, but the tide caught our warp and gave us a sheer that brought us much too close alongside of her. When the sea took her she seemed to hang right over us, and the sight of that great dark hull, looking as if, when it fell, it must come right atop of us, made us want to sheer off, I can tell you. I sung out, " Have you seen the ship ? " And one of the men bawled back, " Yes." " How does she bear ? " " Nor'-west by north." " Have you seen anything go to her ? " The answer I caught was, " A boat." Some of our men said the answer was, " A lifeboat," but most of us only heard, " A boat."

' The tug was now towing ahead, and we went past the lightship, but ten minutes after Tom Friend sings out, " They're burning a light aboard her ! " and looking astern I saw they had fired a red signal light that was blazing over the bulwark in a long shower of sparks. The tug put her helm down to return, and we were brought broadside to the sea. Then we felt the power of those waves, sir. It looked a wonder that we were not rolled over and drowned, every man of us. We held on with our teeth clenched, and twice the boat was filled, and the water up to our throats. " Look out for it, men ! " was always the cry. But every upward send emptied the noble little craft, like pulling out a plug in a wash-basin, and in a few minutes we were again alongside the light-vessel. This time there were six or seven men looking over the side. " What do you want? " we shouted. " Did you see the Sunk lightship's rocket ? " they all yelled out together. " Yes. Did you say you saw a boat ? " " No," they answered, showing we had mistaken their first reply. On which I shouted to the tug, "Pull us round to the Long Sand Head buoy!" and then we were under weigh again, meeting the tremendous seas. There was only a little bit of moon, westering fast, and what there was of it showed but now and again, as the heavy clouds opened and let the light of it down. Indeed, it was very dark, though there was some kind of glimmer in the foam which enabled us to mark the tug ahead. " Bitter cold work, Charlie," says old Tom Cooper to me: " but," says he, " it's colder for the poor wretches aboard the wreck, if they're alive to feel it." The thought of them made our own sufferings small, and we kept look-ing and looking into the darkness around, but there was nothing to be spied, only now and again and long whiles apart the flash of a rocket in the sky from the Sunk lightship. Meanwhile, from time to time, we burnt a hand-signal—a light, sir, that's fired something after the manner of a gun. You fit it into a wooden tube, and give a sort of hammer at the end a smart blow, and the flame rushes out, and a bright light it makes, sir. Ours were green lights, and whenever I set one flaring I couldn't help taking notice of the appearance of the men. It was a queer sight, I assure you, to see them all as green as leaves, with their cork jackets swelling out their bodies so as scarcely to seem like human beings, and the black water as high as our mast-head, or howling a long way below us, on either side. They burned hand-signals on the tug, too, but nothing came of them. There was no sign of the wreck, and staring over the edge of the boat, with the spray and the darkness, was like trying to see through the bottom of a well.

' So we began to talk the matter over, and Tom Cooper

says, "We had better stop here and wait for daylight."
" I'm for stopping," says Steve Goldsmith; and Bob
Penny says, "We're here to fetch the wreck, and fetch
it we will, if we wait a week." "Right," says I; and all
hands being agreed—without any fuss, sir, though I dare
say most of our hearts were at home, and our wishes
alongside our hearths, and the warm fires in them—we
all of us put our hands to our mouths and made one
great cry of "Vulcan ahoy!" The tug dropped astern.
"What do you want?" sings out the skipper, when he
gets within speaking distance. "There's nothing to be
seen of the vessel, so we had better lie-to for the night,"
I answered. "Very good," he says, and then the steamer,
without another word from her crew, and the water
tumbling over her bows like cliffs, resumed her station
ahead, her paddles revolving just fast enough to keep
her from dropping astern.

'As coxswain of the lifeboat, sir, I take no credit for
resolving to lie-to all night. But I am bound to say a
word for the two crews, who made up their minds without a murmur, without a second's hesitation, to face the
bitter cold and fierce seas of that long winter darkness,
that they might be on the spot to help their fellow-
creatures when the dawn broke and showed them where
they were. I know there are scores of sailors round our
coasts who would have done likewise. Only read, sir,
what was done in the North, Newcastle way, during the
gales last October. But surely, sir, no matter who may
be the men who do what they think their duty, whether
they belong to the North or the South, they deserve the
encouragement of praise. A man likes to feel, when he
has done his best, that his fellow-men think well of his

work. If I had not been one of that crew I should wish to say more ; but no false pride shall make me say less, sir, and I thank God for the resolution He put into us, and for the strength He gave us to keep that resolution.

'All that we had to do now was to make ourselves as comfortable as we could. Our tow-rope veered us out a long way, too far astern of the tug for her to help us as a breakwater, and the manner in which we were flung towards the sky with half our keel out of water and then dropped into a hollow—like falling from the top of a house, sir,—while the heads of the seas blew into and tumbled over us all the time, made us all reckon that, so far from getting any rest, most of our time would be spent in preventing ourselves from being washed overboard. We turned to and got the foresail aft, and made a kind of roof of it. This was no easy job, for the wind was so furious that wrestling even with that bit of a sail was like fighting with a steam-engine. When it was up ten of us snugged ourselves away under it, and two men stood on the after-grating thwart keeping a look-out, with the life-lines around them. As you know, sir, we carry a binnacle, and the lamp in it was alight and gave out just enough haze for us to see each other in. We all lay in a lump together for warmth, and a fine show we made, I dare say ; for a cork jacket, even when a man stands upright, isn't calculated to improve his figure, and as we all of us had cork jackets on and oil-skins, and many of us sea boots, you may guess what a raffle of legs and arms we showed, and what a rum heap of odds and ends we looked, as we sprawled in the bottom of the boat upon one another. Sometimes it would be Johnny Goldsmith—for we had three Goldsmiths—Steve

and Dick and Johnny—growling underneath that some-
body was lying on his leg ; and then maybe Harry Meader
would bawl out that there was a man sitting on his head ;
and once Tom Friend swore his arm was broke: but my
opinion is, sir, that it was too cold to feel inconveniences
of this kind, and I believe that some among us would
not have known if their arms and legs really had been
broke, until they tried to use 'em, for the cold seemed to
take away all feeling out of the blood.

'As the seas flew over the boat the water filled the sail
that was stretched overhead and bellied it down upon us,
and that gave us less room, so that some had to lie flat
on their faces ; but when this bellying got too bad we'd
all get up and make one heave with our backs under the
sail, and chuck the water out of it in that way. "Charlie
Fish," says Tom Cooper to me, in a grave voice, "what
would some of them young gen'lmen as comes to Ramsgate in the summer, and says they'd like to go out in the
lifeboat, think of this?" This made me laugh, and then
young Tom Cooper votes for another nipper of rum all
round ; and as it was drawing on for one o'clock in the
morning, and some of the men were groaning with cold,
and pressing themselves against the thwarts with the
pain of it, I made no objection, and the liquor went
round. I always take a cake of Fry's chocolate with me
when I go out in the lifeboat, as I find it very support-
ing, and I had a mind to have a mouthful now; but
when I opened the locker I found it full of water, my
chocolate nothing but paste, and the biscuit a mass of
pulp. This was rather hard, as there was nothing else
to eat, and there was no getting near the tug in that sea
unless we wanted to be smashed into staves. However,

we hadn't come out to enjoy ourselves; nothing was said, and so we lay in a heap, hugging one another for warmth, until the morning broke.

'The first man to look to leeward was old Tom's son —young Tom Cooper—and in a moment he bawled out, "There she is!" pointing like a madman. The morning had only just broke, and the light was grey and dim, and down in the west it still seemed to be night; the air was full of spray, and scarcely were we a-top of a sea than we were rushing like an arrow into the hollow again, so that young Tom must have had eyes like a hawk to have seen her. Yet the moment he sung out and pointed, all hands cried out, "There she is!" But what was it, sir? Only a mast about three miles off—just one single mast sticking up out of the white water, as thin and faint as a spider's line. Yet that was the ship we had been waiting all night to see. There she was, and my heart thumped in my ears the moment my eye fell on that mast. But Lord, sir, the fearful sea that was raging between her and us! for where we were was deepish water, and the waves regular; but all about the wreck was the Sand, and the water on it was running in fury all sorts of ways, rushing up in tall columns of foam as high as a ship's mainyard, and thundering so loudly that, though we were to windward, we could hear it above the gale and the boiling of the seas around us. It might have shook even a man who wanted to die to look at it, if he didn't know what the Bradford can go through.

'I ran my eye over the men's faces. "Let slip the tow rope," bawled Dick Goldsmith. "Up foresail," I shouted, and two minutes after we had sighted that mast we were dead before the wind, our storm foresail taut as a drum-

THE LIFEBOAT BRADFORD AT THE WRECK OF THE INDIAN CHIEF.

Q

skin, our boat's stem heading full for the broken seas
and the lonely stranded vessel in the midst of them.
It was well that there was something in front of us to
keep our eyes that way, and that none of us thought of
looking astern, or the sight of the high and frightful
seas which raged after us might have played old Harry
with weak nerves. Some of them came with such force
that they leapt right over the boat, and the air was dark
with water flying a dozen yards high over us in broad
solid sheets, which fell with a roar like the explosion
of a gun ten or a dozen fathoms ahead. But we took
no notice of these seas, even when we were in the thick
of the broken waters, and all the hands holding on to
the thwarts for dear life. Every thought was upon the
mast that was growing bigger and clearer, and sometimes
when a sea hove us high we could just see the hull,
with the water as white as milk flying over it. The mast
was what they call ' bright,' that is, scraped and varnished,
and we knew that if there was anything living aboard
that doomed ship we should find it on that mast ; and
we strained our eyes with all our might, but could see
nothing that looked like a man. But on a sudden I
caught sight of a length of canvas streaming out of the
top, and all of us seeing it we raised a shout, and a few
minutes after we saw the men. They were all dressed
in yellow oilskins, and the mast being of that colour was
the reason why we did not see them sooner. They
looked a whole mob of people, and one of us roared out,
" All hands are there, men ! " and I answered, " Aye, the
whole ship's company, and we'll have them all ! " for
though, as we afterwards knew, there were only eleven of
them, yet, as I have said, they looked a great number

huddled together in that top, and I made sure the whole ship's company were there.

'By this time we were pretty close to the ship, and a fearful wreck she looked, with her mainmast and mizzen-mast gone, and her bulwarks washed away, and great lumps of timber and planking ripping out of her and going overboard with every pour of the seas. We let go our anchor fifteen fathoms to windward of her, and as we did so we saw the poor fellows unlashing themselves and dropping one by one over the top into the lee rigging. As we veered out cable and drove down under her stern, I shouted to the men on the wreck to bend a piece of wood on to a line and throw it overboard for us to lay hold of. They did this, but they had to get aft first, and I feared for the poor half-perished creatures again and again as I saw them scrambling along the lee rail, stopping and holding on as the mountainous seas swept over the hull, and then creeping a bit further aft in the pause. There was a horrible muddle of spars and torn canvas and rigging under her lee, but we could not guess what a fearful sight was there until our hawser having been made fast to the wreck, we had hauled the lifeboat close under her quarter. There looked to be a whole score of dead bodies knocking about among the spars. It stunned me for a moment, for I had thought all hands were in the foretop, and never dreamt of so many lives having been lost. Seventeen were drowned, and there they were, most of them, and the body of the captain lashed to the head of the mizzenmast, so as to look as if he were leaning over it, his head stiff upright and his eyes watching us, and the stir of the seas made him appear to be struggling to get to us. I thought he

CHARLES FISH,
LATE COXSWAIN OF THE RAMSGATE LIFEBOAT

was alive, and cried to the men to hand him in, but someone said he was killed when the mizzenmast fell, and had been dead four or five hours. This was a dreadful shock; I never remember the like of it. I can't hardly get those fixed eyes out of my sight, sir, and I lie awake for hours of a night, and so does Tom Cooper, and others of us, seeing those bodies torn by the spars and bleeding, floating in the water alongside the miserable ship.

'Well, sir, the rest of this lamentable story has been told by the mate of the vessel, and I don't know that I could add anything to it. We saved the eleven men, and I have since heard that all of them are doing well. If I may speak, as coxswain of the lifeboat, I would like to say that all hands concerned in this rescue, them in the tug as well as the crew of the boat, did what might be expected of English sailors—for such they are, whether you call some of them boatmen or not; and I know in my heart, and say it without fear, that from the hour of leaving Ramsgate Harbour to the moment when we sighted the wreck's mast, there was only one thought in all of us, and that was that the Almighty would give us the strength and direct us how to save the lives of the poor fellows to whose assistance we had been sent.'

Ten years more fly by, in which there is a splendid record of services and rescues to the credit of Coxswain Fish, the Ramsgate lifeboatmen, and the brave steam-tugs, Vulcan and Aid, and we come to the night of Jan. 5 and 6, 1891, which is exactly, my readers will see, ten years to the day after the rescue of the survivors of the Indian Chief, a rescue certainly unsurpassed for its dramatic intensity and its heroism even by the Deal lifeboat.

At 3 a m. on the night of Jan. 5, 1891, Coxswain Fish was asleep in his hammock in the watch-house at the end of Ramsgate pier. There was a gale blowing from the E.N.E., and in the long frost of that awful winter there was no more terrible night than this. The thermometer stood at 15° below freezing-point ; there was a great sea and strong wind.

At 3 a.m. Fish was called by the watch on Ramsgate pier, and he saw a flare on the Goodwins through the rifts in the snow squall. At 2.15 Richard Roberts, the coxswain of the Deal lifeboat, was also roused from sleep and launched his lifeboat, manned by the gallant Deal men. But though the Deal men launched at 2.15 a.m., they had not the same favourable chance of reaching the wreck, beating eight miles dead to windward, as compared with the Ramsgate lifeboat, towed into the eye of the wind by its powerful steam-tug Aid.

We may on this occasion, therefore, leave out the consideration of the Deal lifeboat, splendid as its effort was, inasmuch as it only arrived at the scene of the wreck just as the Ramsgate lifeboat had saved the crew. Some of the hardy Deal lifeboatmen were almost benumbed and rendered helpless by the cold, and they only saw the tragedy of the captain's death and the rescue of the remainder of the crew from the wreck by the Ramsgate men.

At 3 a.m. then the Ramsgate rocket went up in answer to the signals from the Gull lightship ; on that bitter night the lifeboat was manned in eight minutes. The lifebelts and oilskins were handed into the lifeboat ;

shivering, the brave hearts got their clothes on, and in less time than this page has been written, the tow rope had been passed into the lifeboat from the Aid, and that tug was out of the harbour, dragging the lifeboat, head to sea, 120 yards astern of her.

It was black midnight, and no man in the boat could see his neighbour; the pier was like a great iceberg and sheeted with ice; the sea was flying over the oilclad figures in the lifeboat and freezing almost as it fell, rattling against the sails or on the deck, or fiercely hurled into the faces of the men; indeed, every oilskin jacket was frozen stiff before they had been towed a quarter of a mile against the furious sea, which drenched them 'like spray,' as the coxswain expressed it, 'from the parish fire engines.' The brave fellows were more than drenched—they were all but frozen, but no one dreamed of turning back, for though the lightship's rockets had stopped they could see the piteous flares from the distant wreck now and then, as the snow squalls broke, beckoning them on.

The vessel on the Goodwins was the three-masted schooner or barquentine The Crocodile, laden with stone from Guernsey to London, and when about a mile or so north of the Goodwins 'reaching' on the port tack, 'missed stays' in the heavy sea, and before they had time to 'wear' ship, she struck the northern face of the Goodwins, against which a tremendous sea was driven by the black north-easter that was blowing from the Pole. She struck the Goodwins bows on with her head to the south-east, and she heeled over to starboard, the sea which rolled from the E.N.E. beating nearly on her port broadside.

The wrecked crew knew their position, and that their only chance was the advent of some lifeboat, and they burned flares, which consisted on this occasion of their own clothes, which they tore off and soaked in oil. They were soon beaten off the deck as the tide rose, and in the darkness had to take to the rigging, the captain, who was an elderly man, and his crew all together climbing in the mizzen weather rigging. The weather rigging was of course more upright than the lee rigging, which leaned over to the right or starboard hand as the vessel lay.

As the tug bored to windward and rapidly neared the vessel they could see the flares being carried up the rigging by the sorely beset crew, and knew the extremity of the case ; then the next snow squall wrapped them in like a winding-sheet, and all was shut out. But still, on plunged the Aid at great speed, for the new tug-boat Aid is a much faster and more powerful boat than either of the old tugs, the Aid and the Vulcan. Towing the lifeboat well to windward of the wreck, at last the moment arrived, and though not a word was spoken and not a signal made, the end of the tow-rope was let go by the lifeboat and sail was made on her for the wrecked vessel, or rather for the flares.

But even then down came an extra furious snow squall, and the lifeboat had to anchor, lest she should miss the vessel altogether.

This took time. Again in the fury of the storm the word was given ' Up anchor ! ' and ' Run down closer to the wreck ! ' and again the anchor was dropped to the best of the judgment of the coxswain. Fish and Cooper were first and second coxswains ten years before, and exactly ten years before to the day and hour the same brave men were in a similar desperate struggle at the wreck of the Indian Chief. In the tremendous sea the anchor was for the second time dropped well to windward of the wreck. The hull was under water, and over it the hungry sea broke in pyramids or solid sheets of flying, freezing spray. As they veered out their cable and came towards the wreck bows foremost, for they anchored the lifeboat this time by the stern, they could dimly see the cowering, clinging figures in the rigging. They had to pay out their powerful cable most cautiously, for great rollers bursting at the top, and the size of a house, every now and then came racing at them, open-mouthed.

I don't believe a man on board remembered it was exactly to the hour ten years since they rescued the crew of the Indian Chief; but their hearts, beating as warmly as ever in the cause of suffering humanity, were concentrated on the present need. They veered down under the stern of the wreck, and passing the cable a little aft in the lifeboat, steered her up under the starboard-quarter of the wreck. They had just got out their grapnel, and were about to throw it into the lee rigging of the wreck, in hopes it would grip and hold—for unless it held of itself no one of the frozen crew could come down to make it fast. Left foot in front, well out on the gunwale, left hand grasping the fore halyards to steady him—strong brave right hand swung back to hurl the grapnel on the next chance, stood a gallant Ramsgate man, when with a roar like the growl of a wild beast, a monstrous sea broke over vessel and lifeboat, not merely filling her up, and over her thwarts, but snapping her strong new Manilla hawser.

Those who know the quality of the splendid cables supplied by the Royal National Lifeboat Institution will understand the great force that must have been exerted to snap this mighty hawser. But so it happened, and away to leeward into the darkness, smothered, baffled, and almost drowned, but by no means beaten, were swept on to and into the shallower and more furious surf of the north-west jaw of the Goodwins, the Ramsgate lifeboatmen.

Contrast the freezing midnight scene of storm and surf, eight miles from the nearest land, with the quiet sleep of millions.

Here was a January midnight, black as a wolf's throat —thermometer 15° below freezing, a mountainous surf on the Goodwins, and only twelve brave men to face it all; but those twelve men were the heroes of a hundred fights, and were determined to save the men on the wreck or die for it.

Therefore, though swept to leeward, they got sail on the lifeboat and got her on the starboard tack, ten men sheeting home the fore sheet. 'Bad job this!' they said, for words were few that night, and they made through the surf for the tug, which was on the look-out for them, and steered for the blue light they burned. Nothing can be more ghastly than the effect of this blue light on the faces of the men or on the wild hurly-burly of boiling snow white foam one moment seen raging round the lifeboat, and the next obliterated in darkness, the more pitchy by reason of the extinguished flare.

The blue light was seen by the Aid, and she moved to leeward to pick up the lifeboat after she emerged from the breakers. Again the tug-boat passed her hawser on board the lifeboat, and once more towed her to windward to the same position as before ; and once again, burning to save the despairing sailors, the lifeboatmen dropped anchor and veered out their last remaining cable, well-knowing this was the last chance, as they had only the one remaining cable. Tight as a fiddle string was the good hawser, and the howling north-easter hummed its weird tune along its vibrating length, as coil after coil was paid out in the lulls, and the lifeboat came closer and closer, and at last slued right under the starboard quarter of the wreck.

By hand-lights, blue and green, they saw, high up in the air, the unfortunate crew lashed in the weather-rigging, i. e. on the port or left side of the wreck, the side opposite to that under shelter of which they lay. The shelter was a poor one, for great seas broke over the wreck and into the lifeboat on the other side.

The men were lashed half-way up the weather rigging of the mizzenmast, and the lifeboatmen shouted to them to come over and drop into the lifeboat. To do this, they, half-frozen as they were, had to unlash themselves from the weather-rigging and, in the awful cold and darkness, climb up to the mast-head, where the lee-rigging or shrouds met more closely the weather-rigging. Every giant sea shook the wreck ; every billow swayed her masts backwards and forwards so that they 'buckled' like fishing-rods, and the marvel is any man of the be-numbed crew succeeded in getting across from the weather side to the lee-rigging aloft.

It must be borne in mind that the deck was under water and 'raked' by every sea, and that the only possible way of reaching the lifeboat was by going up the rigging from the place where the wrecked crew were lashed, and coming down—if only they could reach across—the other side, which was next the lifeboat, and thence jumping or being hauled into her.

The topsails were in ribbons, and as the wrecked sailors clambered aloft the great whips of torn canvas lashed and terrified and wounded them. By great effort they got across the black gulf between the two riggings —all but the captain.

There high in air—visible as the blue lights flared up from the lifeboat, struggling hard for life, hung the captain.

One leg straddled across the chasm—one hand clutched the weather-rigging he wanted to leave, and one hand reached out blindly—hopefully to catch the lee shrouds—'You'll do it, captain! Come on, captain! For God's sake, captain, come on!' And every face in the blue glare was riveted on the struggling man but,— oh! what anguish to the staring lifeboatmen eager to save him!—he fell, his life-belt being torn off in his fall, full forty feet on to the wave-washed mizzen boom.

'Out boat-hooks, brave hearts, and catch him.' But a great billow broke over the wreck and lifeboatmen, and never was he seen again.

This time death won.

Let us trust he was ready to meet his God. 'If it be not now, yet it will come—the readiness is all.'

Some jumping, and some dragged by the lines, the rest of the shipwrecked men got into the lifeboat, so dazed, so benumbed that they neither realised the loss of the captain nor their own miraculous preservation.

Just at this moment, under press of canvas, the foam flying from her blue bows, at full speed came the Deal lifeboat, too late to avert the disaster they had witnessed.

They had left Deal at 2.15, but not having the aid of steam, were half-frozen and much later on the scene of action than the Ramsgate tug and lifeboat, to whom the honour of this grand rescue belongs.

They reached Ramsgate Harbour at 7.30 a.m. and at 9 o'clock, without having gone ashore to breakfast, almost worn out, but borne up by dauntless spirit within, in response to a telegram from Broadstairs, the same steam-tug, lifeboat, coxswain and crew, again steamed out of Ramsgate Harbour. A collier. the Glide, had gone to the bottom after collision with another vessel, named the Glance—such strange coincidences there are in real life —and the crew of the Glide had taken to their own small ship's boat, while the crew of the Glance had been saved by the Broadstairs lifeboat.

The crew of the Glide in their little boat were in great peril in the mountainous seas which run off the North Foreland in easterly gales, and it was feared they were lost.

Once more into the teeth of the icy gale, without rest and with only snatches of food taken in the lifeboat, after the long exposure of the preceding night and its terrible scenes, the Ramsgate men were towed behind their tug-boat to the rescue. They found the boat of the Glide riding in a furious sea to a sea-anchor, the very best thing they could have done. A sea-anchor may be rigged up by tying sails and oars together, with, if possible, a weight attached just to keep them under water, and then pitching the lot overboard.

To this half-floating, half-submerged mass, the boat's painter was made fast, and as it dragged through the water much more slowly than the boat, the latter checked in its drift came head to sea, and yielding to the send of each wave rode over crests and combers which would otherwise have swamped her.

Hardly hoping for deliverance, they saw the steam-tug and lifeboat making for them and ranging to windward of them to give them a lee, and they were all dragged at last safely into the Bradford. Soon they were towed in between Ramsgate piers, and this time the flying of the British red ensign denoted, 'All saved.' Shouts of rejoicing hailed the double exploit of the hardy lifeboatmen, and their fellow townsmen of Ramsgate proudly felt they had done 'by no means a bad piece of work before breakfast that morning.'

'Storm Warriors' of unconquered Kent, rivals in a hundred deeds of mercy with your brethren the Deal boatmen, and with them sharing the title of 'Heroes of the Goodwin Sands,' God guard you in your perils and bring you safe home at last!

At many other points around the British Isles the same noble spirit is displayed of splendid daring in a sacred cause. Would that all the stalwart fishermen and boatmen of this dear England, as their prototypes of the Sea of Galilee, would serve and follow Him who Himself 'came to seek and to save that which was lost,' that so passing through the waves of this troublesome world, finally they may come through Him to the land of everlasting life!

www.ingramcontent.com/pod-product-compliance
Lightning Source LLC
Chambersburg PA
CBHW030407100426
42812CB00028B/2856/J